WORKBO

ENGLISH 6

Mario Herrera • **Christopher Sol Cruz**

Big English
Workbook 6

Pearson Education, 10 Bank Street, White Plains, NY 10606 USA

Staff credits: The people who made up the *Big English* team, representing editorial, production, design, manufacturing, and marketing are Rhea Banker, Danielle Belfiore, Carol Brown, Tracey Munz Cataldo, Daniel Comstock, Mindy DePalma, Dave Dickey, Gina DiLillo, Christine Edmonds, Nancy Flaggman, Yoko Mia Hirano, Caroline Kasterine, Amy Kefauver, Lucille Kennedy, Penny Laporte, Christopher Leonowicz, Emily Lippincott, Maria Pia Marrella, Jennifer McAliney, Kate McLoughlin, Julie Molnar, Linda Moser, Kyoko Oinuma, Leslie Patterson, Sherri Pemberton, Pamela Pia, Stella Reilly, Nicole Santos, Susan Saslow, Donna Schaffer, Chris Siley, Kim Snyder, Heather St. Clair, Mairead Stack, Katherine Sullivan, Jane Townsend, Kenneth Volcjak, and Lauren Weidenman.

Contributing Writer: Teresa Lintner

Text composition: Bill Smith Group/Q2A Media

Illustration credits: Q2A Media Services, Anthony Lewis

Photo credits: Title/Cover (bc) wow/Shutterstock; 2 (tl) Corbis Super RF/Alamy, (tc) Comstock/Thinkstock, (tr) Ron Nickel/Design Pics Inc./Alamy, (cl) Adrian Sherratt/Alamy, (c) DAJ/amana images inc./Alamy, (cr) Chris Clinton/Getty Images; 3 (cl) Comstock/Thinkstock, (cr) Bonita R. Cheshier/Shutterstock, (bl) Hemera/Thinkstock, (cr) Michey/Kalium/Agefotostock; 4 (tl) Jaimie Duplass/Shutterstock, (cl) Galina Barskaya/Shutterstock, (bl) Monkey Business Images/Shutterstock; 7 (tr) Jupiterimages, Brand X Pictures/Thinkstock; 8 (tr) KRZYSTOF SWIDERSKI/EPA/Newscom; 9 (cr) Vicky Kasala/The Image Bank/Getty Images; 11 (tc) Galina Barskaya/Shutterstock; 12 (tl) Martin Harvey/Alamy, (tc) Image Source/Alamy, (tr) Kiselev Andrey Valerevich/Shutterstock, (cl) Alexander Raths/Shutterstock, (c) goodluz/Fotolia, (cr) Sabphoto/Fotolia; 13 (tr) Jerry Marks Productions/Glow Images; 14 (tr) Dim Dimich/Shutterstock; 17 (tr) i love images/family/Alamy; 18 (tr) GL Archive/Alamy; 19 (tr) Rossillicon Photos/Shutterstock; 21 (tr) AVAVA/Shutterstock; 22 (tl) Peredniankina/Shutterstock, (tc) Catherine Murray/Shutterstock, (tr) Kseniia Perminova/Shutterstock, (cl) Frederic Cirou/PhotoAlto/Alamy, (c) Eléonore H/Fotolia, (cr) Galina Barskaya/Shutterstock; 23 (c) J_Foto/Fotolia, (cr) Robert Crum/Shutterstock; 24 (tr) MANDY GODBEHEAR/Shutterstock; 26 (tr) michaeljung/Shutterstock; 27 (tr) Digital Vision/Thinkstock; 28 (cr) milias1987/Shutterstock; 31 (tc) Hemera/Thinkstock; 32 (bl) Edyta Pawlowska/Shutterstock; 34 (tl) everything possible/Shutterstock, (tc) koya979/Shutterstock, (tr) Andrea Danti/Shutterstock, (cl) I. Glory/Alamy, (blonde girl) S.White/Fotolia, (boy in yellow) Anders Blomqvist/Alamy, (brunette girl) Paul Simcock/Blend Images/Alamy, (boy in red) RC30/Glow Asia RF/Alamy, (girl in purple) Megapress/Alamy; 35 (bkgd) quinky/Shutterstock, (tl) J_Foto/Fotolia, (tr) Creativa/Shutterstock, (c) mangostock/Shutterstock, (br) Andres Rodriguez/Fotolia; 38 (cl) Pamela Mullins/Shutterstock, (cr) Real Deal Photo/Shutterstock; 39 (br) Andres Rodriguez/Fotolia; 40 (cr) Hubis/Shutterstock, (br) Paul Fleet/Shutterstock; 41 (tr) Pressmaster/Shutterstock; 43 (tr) Sergey Nivens/Shutterstock; 44 (tl) Alexandra Petruk/Shutterstock, (tc) David Grigg/Shutterstock, (tr) benchart/Shutterstock, (cl) Danomyte/Shutterstock, (c) bcdan/Shutterstock, (cr) Danomyte/Shutterstock; 48 (cl) Giuseppe_R/Shutterstock, (cr) Tracy Whiteside/Shutterstock, (bl) Blend Images/Shutterstock, (br) Image Source Plus/Alamy; 50 (tl) chawalitpix/Fotolia; 52 (cr) GIGIBGM/Shutterstock; 54 (tl) Sergii Figurnyi/Shutterstock, (tc) Erik Isakson/Blend Images/Alamy, (tr) eddie linssen/Alamy, (cl) Laurin Rinder/Shutterstock, (c) Image Source Plus/Alamy, (cr) Corbis Super RF/Alamy; 55 (tr) Stu Porter/Shutterstock, (tcr) NHPA/SuperStock, (cr) Fine Art Images/AgeFotostock; 56 (tr) Blue Lantern Studio/Corbis; 60 (cr) faizzaki/Fotolia; 63 (tr) Fine Art Images/AgeFotostock; 64 (t) Oleksiy Mark/Shutterstock, (c) ianmurray/Alamy, (b) Corbis Super RF/Alamy; 66 (tl) Sabena Jane Blackbird/Alamy, (tc) Andreas Meyer/Shutterstock, (tr) blickwinkel/Alamy, (cl) DU BOISBERRANGER Jean/hemis.fr/Hemis/Alamy, (c) Beinecke Rare Book and Manuscript Library/Yale University; 67 (tl) PiLensPhoto/Fotolia, (cl) feferoni/Fotolia; 68 (tr) Beinecke Rare Book and Manuscript Library/Yale University; 71 (cr) Monkey Business Images/Shutterstock; 73 (tr) patrimonio designs ltd/Shutterstock; 75 (tr) Enno Kleinert/dieKleinert/Alamy; 76 (tl) KaYann/Fotolia, (tc) Matthew Jacques/Shutterstock, (tr) Iva/Fotolia, (cl) ILYA GENKIN/Alamy, (c) Aleksandar Todorovic/Shutterstock, (cr) chungking/Shutterstock; 77 (tl) Subbotina Anna/Fotolia, (tc) Phon Promwisate/Shutterstock, (tr) Nestor Noci/Shutterstock, (cl) Somchai Som/Shutterstock, (c) Nella/Shutterstock, (cr) Walter Bibikow/Jon Arnold Images Ltd/Alamy; 78 (tr) Jon Arnold Images Ltd/Alamy; 80 (tr) M Reel/Shutterstock; 81 (c) KaYann/Fotolia; 82 (tr) dwori/Shutterstock; 83 (tr) Subbotina Anna/Fotolia; 86 (tl) Stefano Amantini/Corbis, (tr) Kzenon/Shutterstock; 87 (tl) Sandy Huffaker/Corbis, (tc) dwphotos/Shutterstock, (tr) Ricardo Maynard/Corbis; 90 (tr) Anna Omelchenko/Shutterstock; 91 (tc) OJO Images Ltd/Alamy; 92 (cr) INTERFOTO/Alamy; 93 (tr) DIETER NAGL/Staff/AFP/Getty Images; 95 (tr) Jeff Morgan 14/Alamy; 96 (tc) PiLensPhoto/Fotolia, (tcr) DU BOISBERRANGER Jean/hemis.fr/Hemis/Alamy, (tr) Enno Kleinert/dieKleinert/Alamy, (cl) Phon Promwisate/Shutterstock, (c) Nestor Noci/Shutterstock, (cr) Subbotina Anna/Fotolia, (bc) Jeff Morgan 14/Alamy, (bcr) Yuri Arcurs/Shutterstock, (br) Yuri Arcurs/Shutterstock; 99 (tr) Christopher Sol Cruz/Sun Cross Media; 100 (tr) Erik Isakson/RubberBall/Alamy; 101 (tl) Robert Crum/Shutterstock, (tcl) bst2012/Fotolia; 103 (tr) silver-john/Shutterstock; 104 (br) Linda Whitwam/DK Images; 105 (tr) Somchai Som/Shutterstock; 106 (tr) egd/Shutterstock; 107 (bc) mocker_bat/Fotolia; 108 (tl) Jason Merritt/Staff/Getty Images, (cl) Speedfighter/Fotolia

Printed in the United States of America

ISBN-10: 0-13-304524-2
ISBN-13: 978-0-13-3045246

Contents

BIG ENGLISH
♪ Song ♪

From the mountaintops to the bottom of the sea,
From a big blue whale to a baby bumblebee—
If you're big, if you're small, you can have it all,
And you can be anything you want to be!

It's bigger than you. It's bigger than me.
There's so much to do, and there's so much to see!
The world is big and beautiful, and so are we!
Think big! Dream big! Big English!

So in every land, from the desert to the sea,
We can all join hands and be one big family.
If we love, if we care, we can go anywhere!
The world belongs to everyone; it's ours to share.

It's bigger than you. It's bigger than me.
There's so much to do, and there's so much to see!
The world is big and beautiful, and so are we!
Think big! Dream big! Big English!

It's bigger than you. It's bigger than me.
There's so much to do, and there's so much to see!
The world is big and beautiful and waiting for me . . .
    a one, two, three . . .
Think big! Dream big! Big English!

unit 1 ALL ABOUT SCHOOL

1 What school activities do you see in the pictures? Write the number.

___ enjoying a field trip

___ working on computers

___ doing a project

___ giving a presentation

___ taking a test

___ practicing yoga

2 Read and check (✓). What would you like your school to have?

	lots of	some	none
1. free time	☐	☐	☐
2. homework	☐	☐	☐
3. tests	☐	☐	☐
4. group projects	☐	☐	☐
5. after-school clubs	☐	☐	☐
6. independent work	☐	☐	☐
7. field trips	☐	☐	☐
8. computers	☐	☐	☐

3 Check (✓) the verbs you use with each phrase. Then listen and check your answers.

	do	study for	turn in	finish	take
1. a test					
2. an assignment					
3. a book report					
4. homework					
5. a project					

4 Read. What should each student have done? Match the name and the advice.
Write the letter.

I finished my writing assignment, but my puppy ate it when I wasn't looking.

Selena

Someone took my book on the bus yesterday. I can't hand in my book report.

Mario

I didn't start my project until yesterday. I couldn't finish it last night.

Tatiana

I wanted to study for the test, but I started playing video games. And then it was too late. My mom told me to go to bed.

Derrick

___ **1.** Selena

___ **2.** Mario

___ **3.** Tatiana

___ **4.** Derrick

a. should have paid attention to the time.

b. should have done it over again.

c. should have done it earlier.

d. should have been more careful.

5 Complete the sentences with an excuse or some advice.

1. **A:** Benji hasn't finished his research project because he started it yesterday.

   B: He _____.

2. **A:** Richie _____.

   B: He should have been more careful.

Reading | Web forum

6 **Listen and read. Circle *True* or *False*.**

ninja_fly

Hey, everyone! What's up? I need your advice. I'm having a problem with my mom. My mom has volunteered for every dance, every field trip, and every fundraiser we've had at school so far this year. Sometimes I like it. But you know what? Kids make fun of me because she is always here. It's embarrassing. I know she thinks the school needs her help, but I need her help too . . . to stay away. What should I do?

free_mind09

OK, ninja_fly. I hear you. It can be really annoying to have your mom at school all the time. You should tell her how you feel. Ask her to stop volunteering for everything and stop coming to school so often. I had the same problem with my mom and it worked for me.

2good_for_u

I agree with free_mind09. You should tell your mom that it bothers you when she comes to school so often. But I don't think she should stop volunteering. I'll bet she likes it, and the school needs it. You should be glad she wants to help. You should tell her that she's an awesome mom, but you would like her to volunteer at school less often. Think positively!

1. Ninja_fly's mom volunteers too much at his school. **True** **False**
2. Both free_mind09 and 2good_for_u think ninja_fly should tell his mom to stop volunteering. **True** **False**
3. Free_mind09 had the same problem with her mom. **True** **False**
4. 2good_for_u thinks volunteering is good. **True** **False**

7 **Answer the question.**

If your mom volunteered, would you feel the same way as ninja_fly? Why or why not?

_____

_____

8 Listen and read. Circle the correct answer.

Jim:	Hey, Carlos. Have you met the new exchange student yet?
Carlos:	No. Why?
Jim:	She's from Finland, and she's really nice!
Carlos:	Nice, <u>huh</u>? Is she smart, too?
Jim:	Really smart. I've talked to her.
Carlos:	In English?
Jim:	Of course in English. But maybe I'll start learning Finnish now.
Carlos:	<u>You're crazy</u>. You haven't even mastered English yet.
Jim:	Finnish is different. I'm sure I'll learn it fast. I'm motivated!
Carlos:	<u>Yeah, yeah, yeah.</u>

1. Carlos **has seen / hasn't seen** the exchange student.

2. Jim **has already talked / hasn't talked** to the exchange student.

3. The exchange student **speaks / doesn't speak** English.

4. Jim **wants / doesn't want** to speak Finnish to the exchange student.

9 Look at 8. Circle the correct answer.

1. When Carlos says "Nice, huh?" the word "huh" means that he's ___.

   a. not interested   **b.** interested

2. "You're crazy" means ___.

   a. what you're saying doesn't make any sense   **b.** what you're saying makes sense

3. The expression "yeah, yeah, yeah" means ___.

   a. I like what you say   **b.** I don't believe that you will do what you say

10 Complete the dialogues. Circle the correct expression. Then listen to check your answers.

1. **A:** I'm going to stop playing video games forever!

   B: No way! **Huh? / You're crazy!** You've played video games ever since I met you.

2. **A:** Jeffrey hasn't asked anyone to the dance yet.

   B: He hasn't, **yeah, yeah, yeah. / huh?** I wonder who he'll ask.

3. **A:** This time I'm going to turn in my project on time.

   B: **You're crazy. / Yeah, yeah, yeah.** That's what you always say, but you're always late.

Grammar

Has she done her solo yet?	Yes, she has. She has already done it.
	No, she hasn't. She hasn't done it yet.
Have they ever won an award?	Yes, they have./No, they haven't.

11 Read about Michael and Ted. Then write the answers or questions.

Michael and Ted's Social Studies Project

 **8:45 PM** Michael and Ted are playing video games. They haven't started their social studies project.

 **2:00 AM** Michael has finished making the model pyramid, but Ted hasn't finished his research yet.

 **8:15 AM** Michael and Ted have finished their project. Ted has fallen asleep.

1. It's 8:45 P.M. Have Michael and Ted gotten supplies for their project yet?
   Yes, they have. They've already gotten supplies for their project.

2. It's 8:45 P.M. Has Michael completed the model of the pyramid yet?
   _____

3. It's 2:00 A.M. Has Ted started doing research on the computer yet?
   _____

4. It's 2:00 A.M. Have Michael and Ted finished their project yet?
   _____

5. It's 8:15 A.M. _____
   Yes, they have. Michael and Ted have already arrived in class.

6. It's 8:30 A.M. _____
   Yes, they have. Michael and Ted have turned in their project.

He **has** already **finished** the project.	He **finished** it yesterday.
He **hasn't finished** the project yet.	He **didn't finish** it yesterday.

12 Look at Sarita's to-do list. Then complete the sentences.

1. Sarita ___made___ posters for the art fair at 4:00.
2. She ___has___ already ___made___ posters for the art fair.
3. Sarita _____ her book report at 5:30.
4. She _____ already _____ her book report.
5. Sarita _____ her science project yet.
6. Sarita _____ her science project tonight.

> **Things to do:**
>
> 1. Make posters for art fair at 4:00 ✔
> 2. Start book report at 5:30 ✔
> 3. Finish science project tonight ☐

13 Complete the dialogues. Use the correct form of the verbs in parentheses.

1. (go)

   A: Has Cathy _____ to dance class yet?

   B: Yes, she _____ to dance class at 3:00.

2. (do)

   A: Has Manuel _____ the laundry yet?

   B: No, he _____ the laundry yet.

3. (turn in)

   A: Has Trudie _____ her homework yet?

   B: No, she _____ her homework yet.

4. (eat)

   A: Has Sean _____ dinner yet?

   B: Yes, he _____ dinner at 6:00.

14 Complete the sentences. Circle the correct form of the verb.

1. I **have finished / finished** my assignment last night, but I **haven't turned / didn't turn** it over yet.

2. Jan **has already taken / took** the test yesterday, but she **has studied / didn't study** for it. She should have studied more.

3. We **haven't started / didn't start** our project yet. We **haven't had / didn't have** time yesterday.

15 Read. Then complete the sentences with the words in the box.

School in Poland

   Do you like taking tests? Then you wouldn't like
going to elementary school in Poland. Students don't
take tests until the end of sixth grade and they do not
get grades for the first three years of school. Would
you like that? That doesn't mean that students don't
learn. They are busy learning about many subjects.
In Poland, students study the following subjects: art,
modern foreign language (like German or English),
gym (PE), music, history, civics, science, math, Polish
language, technology, and computer science. Also, each week students get one period
with a tutor who helps them with their schoolwork. How many subjects do you study?
Would you like that extra help?

   In 1999, the Polish government made changes in the education system because
students' scores were low. Students began to spend more time reading and studying
their language. This has made a big difference in students' performance on tests. Daily
homework is only about a half-hour. That gives students more free time. Students do not
complain about that! Would you?

> daily   free time   period   schedule

1. Most students are happy with less homework and more _____.

2. Each student studies language and math _____.

3. A free _____ for extra help would benefit every student at every school.

4. A typical _____ in Poland includes computer science and civics.

16 How does the school in Poland compare with your school?

1. Write one sentence about how it is different.

_____

_____

2. Write one sentence about how it is similar.

_____

_____

17 Read. Circle *True* or *False*.

Education in Finland, China, and Poland is different in some ways, but students in all these countries do well on achievement tests. Finland has the highest scores in science, math, and reading, yet students go to school for only four hours a day on average. That's pretty amazing! Students in Poland are in school a little longer. In China, students are in school from 8 to 11 hours a day.

Class size is also different. In Finland, classes are small. The average class size is 18. Classes in Poland are even smaller. In China, they are much larger. The way the school day is structured is different too. Students in China and Poland follow schedules, but in Finland students decide what they want to do each day. The teacher gives them choices and the students decide.

Students in China spend the most time at home completing assignments. But students in all three of these countries don't do a lot of homework. Is homework important? People have very different opinions on this topic. The interesting thing is that students in these countries learn a lot without doing a lot of homework. They have more time to enjoy learning about things outside of the classroom. Do you think that is the reason their test scores are so high?

	Finland	China	Poland
How many hours of school?	4	8 – 11	6 ½
How large are classes?	18	37	12
Is there a schedule?	No	Yes	Yes
How much time do students spend doing homework each day?	half-hour daily	one-hour daily	half-hour daily

1. Children in China spend more time in school than children in Poland.   **True**   **False**

2. Class size is the largest in Poland.   **True**   **False**

3. Students in Finland have a strict school schedule.   **True**   **False**

4. There are many hours of homework in Finland and Poland.   **True**   **False**

18 Write the answer.

If you could choose subjects to study, what would you choose? Why?

_____

_____

Writing | Paragraph of Opinion

In an opinion paragraph, you share your opinion about a topic. To write an opinion paragraph, follow these steps:

- Write your opinion. Use your opinion as the title of your opinion paragraph. For example:

  Longer School Days Will Not Improve Grades

- To begin your opinion paragraph, rewrite the title of your paragraph as a question. Then answer the question with your opinion:

  Will longer school days improve grades? In my opinion, they won't.

- Next, write reasons for your opinion:

  Students will be too tired after a longer school day to do their homework. They will have less time to work on school projects and study for tests.

- Then, write suggestions:

  I think offering after-school tutoring for students who need extra help is a better idea. Teachers could also assign more group projects. That way, students could help each other while they complete school assignments.

- Finally, write a conclusion:

  In my opinion, offering extra help to students and assigning more group projects are better ideas than having longer school days. Longer school days will just cause stress. They might even cause students to do poorly at school because they will be tired and less motivated.

19 **Choose one of the school issues below.**

- Students should/shouldn't use cell phones in school.
- It is important /It is not important to use computers in the classroom.

State your opinion here: _____

20 **Write an outline for your topic in 19. Complete the chart below:**

Title rewritten as question:
Main opinion:
Reason:
Suggestion:
Conclusion:

21 **Write an opinion paragraph on a separate piece of paper. Use your information from 20.**

22 Read. Unscramble the questions. Use the present perfect form of the verbs. Then complete the answers.

DONE
Do my social studies homework

Finish my science project

Anna

NOT DONE
Study for math test

1. yet / Anna / do / social studies homework

   Q: *Has Anna done her social studies homework yet?*

   A: *Yes, she has already done her social studies homework.*

2. study for / math test / her / she / yet

   Q: _____

   A: _____

3. she / finish / yet / science project / her

   Q: _____

   A: _____

23 Complete the sentences. Use the correct form of the verbs in parentheses.

1. Mark _____ (study) for his math test yesterday.

2. Sarah _____ (finish) her book report last week.

3. Juan _____ (turn in, not) his English assignment yet.

4. Marissa _____ already _____ (do) her homework.

24 Write the answer.

Ted didn't hand in his writing assignment because he fell asleep and didn't finish. What should he have done? Choose the best idea in the box. Add an idea of your own.

done it earlier   done it over   paid less attention to the time

_____

_____

unit 2 AMAZING YOUNG PEOPLE

1 Match the pictures to sentences about life dreams. Write the number.

Someday I would like to . . .

☐ create a photography blog

☐ be a professional soccer player

☐ live on a farm

☐ start my own band

☐ see animals in Africa

☐ find a cure for diseases

2 Write down four of your dreams. Rank them by importance. 1 = most important. 4 = least important.

1. _____

2. _____

3. _____

4. _____

3 Look at 2. Which of your dreams will be the most difficult to achieve? Draw a box around it. Which dream will be the easiest to achieve? Underline it. Which dream can you do right now? Write it here:

_____

4 Read. Then circle *True* or *False*.

My parents are amazing people! My mom is a writer. She wrote and published her first book when she was just 14 years old! She also speaks three languages: English, Spanish, and French. My dad is a famous chess player. He has played chess for over 20 years and has won many tournaments. He also plays the piano and the guitar. My parents are amazing people for all their achievements—especially for being wonderful parents to me and my sister!

Our children are amazing kids! Our son Chris is great at science. At just ten years old, he started his own science club. The club meets every Friday after school. Last week, he won an award for his latest invention: a portable mp3 case that protects your mp3 player from getting wet! He wants to be a doctor when he grows up. Emma is a terrific athlete! She's the captain of her soccer and softball team. Her soccer team just won a big soccer tournament. Emma won the Most Valuable Player award! Emma loves being active…her biggest dream is to climb a mountain one day! We are very proud of our amazing kids!

1. Chris's dad has published a book.	**True**	**False**
2. His mom speaks three languages.	**True**	**False**
3. Chris's dad plays two instruments.	**True**	**False**
4. Chris hasn't invented anything yet.	**True**	**False**
5. Emma's team just won a soccer tournament.	**True**	**False**
6. Emma has already climbed a mountain.	**True**	**False**

5 Complete the sentences. Use the words in the box.

> invented something   published a book   speak 23 languages   won a contest   wrote a book

1. Elyse Mancuso, a young girl from Nebraska, _____ on a TV show called Jeopardy. She won more money than any other contestant.

2. Kevin Doe _____ amazing when he was only 13. He made batteries from junk and helped bring electricity to people's homes in Sierra Leone.

3. Timothy Donor taught himself to _____ by the time he was 16.

4. Adora Svitak _____ and _____ about how to write when she was only seven.

6 Write two goals that you have for this school year.

_____

_____

Listen and read. Then answer the questions.

Adora Svitak

by Tracy Doring

Adora Svitak considers herself a writer, a teacher, and an activist. She began writing when she was four years old. She wrote *Flying Fingers* at age seven. In it, she talks about how important writing is and explains how to write. In 2008, Adora published a book of poetry that she co-wrote with her sister.

Adora says that when she hears kids say that reading and writing are not very important in their lives, she gets upset. She thinks that reading and writing about ideas can help change the world. In 2010, Adora gave a presentation titled "What Adults Can Learn from Kids." She said that adults need to think like kids because kids think optimistically and creatively when solving problems. She mentioned kids like Ruby Bridges, who helped end segregation in the United States. Adults, on the other hand, think of limitations and problems.

Adora continues to publish her work and give speeches. In 2011, she published her first full-length novel, *Yang in Disguise*. In 2012, Adora won an award given by the National Press Club. At the awards ceremony, she gave a speech about the importance of girls achieving their goals and living their dreams. One of Adora's goals is to win a Nobel Prize.

Adora believes that the way to change the world is to trust kids and expect that they will do great things at a young age. Parents and teachers, she says, have low expectations of students. They don't expect kids to achieve much. They expect kids to listen, and not show their brilliance. This thinking has to change. She says that adults should expect wonderful things and learn to listen to kids. The future depends on it.

1. What is one of Adora's accomplishments?

_____

2. What is one of Adora's future goals?

_____

3. How does Adora believe the world should change?

_____

4. Do you agree or disagree with Adora? Explain your answer.

_____

8 Listen. Circle *True* or *False*.

Jenn: Felipe, what's your brother doing on his computer? I can see he's really <u>getting into it</u>.

Felipe: He's probably working on one of his computer programs.

Jenn: He writes computer programs? But he's only 12!

Felipe: I know. He started writing programs when he was about 9.

Jenn: 9? That's incredible.

Felipe: He's in trouble with my parents, though. He wants to <u>drop out</u> of school and work on his programs all day.

Jenn: <u>You're joking</u>, right?

Felipe: Yeah, I'm <u>just kidding</u>.

1. Felipe's brother likes computers a lot.   **True**   **False**

2. His brother started working with computers when he was in his teens.   **True**   **False**

3. His parents don't like their children to spend a lot of time on the computer.   **True**   **False**

4. Felipe's brother is going to stop going to school.   **True**   **False**

9 Look at **8**. Read the underlined expressions. Match the expressions with the meaning. Write the letter.

___ **1.** get into   **a.** say something funny to make people laugh

___ **2.** drop out   **b.** say something surprising that doesn't sound possible

___ **3.** be joking   **c.** stop going before you finish

___ **4.** be kidding   **d.** become interested in

10 Answer the questions.

1. Have you ever dropped out of a class or a club? What was it? Why did you drop out?

_____

2. Are you getting into something interesting this year? What is it? Why do you like it?

_____

3. Look at **8**. Why did Jenn say, "You're joking"?

_____

Grammar

How long **has** she **played** the piano?
She**'s played** the piano *for* five years.

How long **have** they **known** about William?
They**'ve known** about William *since* they saw a movie about him.

11 Look and match the phrases to *since* or *for*.

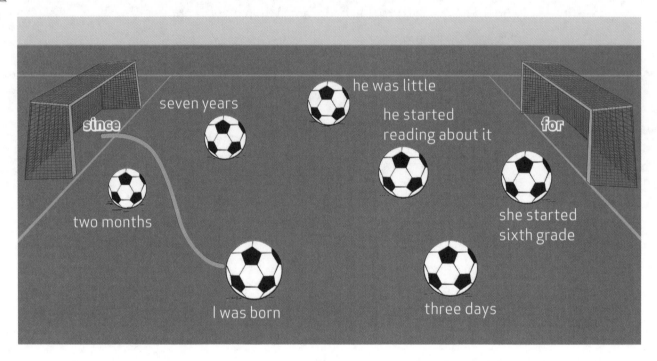

seven years

he was little

he started
reading about it

since

two months

for

she started
sixth grade

I was born

three days

12 Complete the sentences with the present perfect form of the verbs and *for* or *since*.

1. Karine loves to swim. She _____ (swim) competitively _____ she was five.

2. Ray loves to read. He _____ (become) very interested in the Middle Ages _____ he read about it in his social studies class.

3. Francisco is entering a TV game show tournament. He _____ (study) hard _____ three days.

4. Chloe loves animals. She _____ (volunteer) at the animal shelter _____ two months.

How long **has** your brother **been playing** tennis?
He**'s been playing** tennis *since* he was five.

How long **have** you and your sister **been bungee jumping**?
We**'ve been bungee jumping** *for* two years.

13 Read. Answer the questions. Use the present perfect progressive.

At age 12, Bobby and Jenny have their own business. They
started working at their business, called "Kids Biz," when they
were nine. They do chores like mowing the grass and washing
cars. Six months ago Jenny started babysitting, too. They also
volunteer in the community. Bobby started collecting money for
the animal shelter two years ago. He does that every year. Jenny
collects food for the homeless. She started doing that when she
was 11. They both blog, too. They started blogging when they started sixth grade.

1. How long have Bobby and Jenny been working at their business Kids Biz?

   They have been working at their business Kids Biz since they were nine. (since)

2. How long has Jenny been babysitting?

   _____ (for)

3. How long has Bobby been volunteering for the animal shelter?

   _____ (for)

4. How long has Jenny been collecting food for the homeless?

   _____ (since)

5. How long have they been blogging?

   _____ (since)

14 Answer the questions in complete sentences.

1. Think of something you are studying in school. How long have you been studying it?

   _____

2. Think of something you love to do. How long have you been doing it?

   _____

Connections | Social Studies

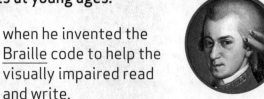

15 Match the amazing people and their accomplishments at young ages.

___ **1.** Mozart composed

___ **2.** At two years old, Aelita Andre created paintings that are so admired by art critics

___ **3.** Fourteen-year-old Nadia Comaneci scored a perfect 10 in gymnastics—

___ **4.** A 12-year-old blind French boy changed the world of reading and writing forever

a. when he invented the <u>Braille</u> code to help the visually impaired read and write.

b. an <u>accomplishment</u> never achieved before at the Olympic Games.

c. that they may become part of museum exhibits for <u>ages</u> to come.

d. a <u>symphony</u> at four and an <u>opera</u> at 14.

16 Unscramble the words and write the letters in the boxes. Look at the words in 15 to help you. There's a message for you. Use the numbers and letters to find the message.

MAMPENHICCTLOS

A	C												

  5   4   12   13

GASE

  8 2

PAEOR

10   3

SYNYPHOM

   9   7

LARLIBE

 1 11   6   14

MESSAGE:

B						Z						U				F	!

 1 2   3 4 5   6 7 8   9 10   11 12 13 14

17 Answer the questions about yourself.

1. Mozart composed symphonies and operas because he loved to create music. What do you like to create?

_____

2. Nadia Comaneci practiced gymnastics every day and was proud of her accomplishments. What accomplishments are you particularly proud of?

_____

18 Read. Then answer the questions.

Imagine a World of Peace

Conflict happens everywhere. It happens in our homes, our schools, our friendships, and our world. When conflict happens, people start to "take sides." To *take sides* means to believe that one person, group, or opinion is completely right and the others are completely wrong. When people take sides, they often do not listen to or hear the other side's concerns or opinions. Do you sometimes feel that someone isn't listening to you when you give your opinion or explain your ideas? How can you encourage people to really listen to you?

Can you imagine a world without conflict? Can you imagine a world where people live together peacefully? Earthdance International can. Earthdance International is an organization that was founded in 1997. Its purpose is to use music and dance to bring people and countries together for peace—especially countries taking sides against each other. Once a year, Earthdance International organizes the Global Festival for Peace. The Festival takes place in different countries around the world, at the same time, on the same day. It is "the largest global synchronized music and peace event in the world." It has taken place in over 80 countries and online! Musicians, singers, dancers, and artists from around the world come together to create song and dance, and talk about peaceful ways to end conflict, injustice, and environmental problems. Everyone enjoys the music and fun, but they are also hard at work discussing ways to make the world a better place. Earthdance International is committed to finding peaceful solutions to difficult problems.

1. Why do people take sides? What happens when they do?

   _____

   _____

2. Earthdance International invites people to get together to talk while dancing and listening to music. Why do you think the organization believes that dancing and music are important for creating peace?

   _____

   _____

3. Would you like to join Earthdance International? Why or why not?

   _____

   _____

In a biography, you write about the important events and details of someone's life. These can include:

- the place where someone was born
- the schools the person went to and what he or she studied
- the jobs the person had
- accomplishments
- important memories and people
- interests

It helps to ask questions and put the events in the correct order.

19 Unscramble the questions. Imagine you are interviewing Stephen Hillenburg, the creator of SpongeBob SquarePants.

1. born? / were / where / you

   You: _____ ?

   Stephen: I was born in Anaheim, California, in 1961.

2. what / study / you / did / in college?

   You: _____ ?

   Stephen: I studied marine biology in college, but I really wanted to study art.
   I got a Master of Fine Arts degree in animation in 1991.

3. are / some / your / what / of / important memories?

   You: _____ ?

   Stephen: When I was young, I loved watching films about the sea. I loved drawing and painting, too.

4. jobs / have / kind of / what / you / had?

   You: _____ ?

   Stephen: I was a marine biologist from 1984–1987. I started working as an animator in 1991.

5. what / your / some of / are / accomplishments?

   You: _____ ?

   Stephen: I have made many films, but my best accomplishment is creating the cartoon SpongeBob SquarePants in 1999. In 2010, it won the Kids' Choice Awards in Mexico, and, in 2012, it won the Kids' Choice Awards in the United States.

20 Write a short biography of Stephen Hillenburg. Use the information in 19. Write two more questions. Do research and find the answers. Add the information to the biography.

21 Complete the paragraphs. Use the present perfect and *for* or *since*.

I have some amazing friends. I _____ (know)
(1)
my friend Anthony _____ we were five years old.
(2)
He _____ (play) chess _____
(3)   (4)
12 years, and he _____ (win) many tournaments.
(5)
I _____ (try) to beat him at a game _____ many
(6)   (7)
years, but I _____ (have, not) any luck! Besides being an amazing
(8)
chess player, Anthony can also speak French! He wants to write and publish a book in

French when he's older.

I _____ (be) friends with Stella _____
(9)   (10)
three years. She is an amazing musician. She _____ (play)
(11)
the piano _____ she was four years old. She also loves
(12)
science. She _____ (be) a member of our school's science club
(13)
_____ over two years. She wants to invent something one day! I am so
(14)
lucky to have such amazing friends!

22 Look at 21. Then answer the questions in complete sentences.

1. Who has won a tournament? _____

2. Who plays an instrument? _____

3. Who speaks another language? _____

4. Who wants to invent something? _____

5. Who wants to write a book? _____

23 Answer the questions. Use the present perfect progressive and *since*.

1. SpongeBob SquarePants started in 1999. How long has it been playing on TV?

_____

2. Seeds of Peace started in 1993. How long has Seeds of Peace been offering its training
   to students?

_____

unit 3 DILEMMAS

1 Look at the photos. How do you think the people are feeling? Write the number on the picture.

1. mad	**4.** guilty	**6.** good about himself or herself
2. worried	**5.** happy	**7.** in trouble
3. upset		

2 Look at 1. What do you think has happened to the people? Why do they look this way? Check the answers. Write your own ideas.

The person . . .

☐ cheated on a test   ☐ heard a hurtful lie

☐ helped a friend at school   ☐ stopped a bully

☐ had a fight with a friend   ☐ _____

☐ _____   ☐ _____

3 Complete the sentences. Circle the correct words.

1. **Kate:** Yesterday, I borrowed my mom's jacket, but I lost it at the park. I don't want her to **get in trouble / be upset** with me so I'm going to tell her that someone took it.

   Sally: Why don't you check the Lost and Found? Maybe someone found the jacket and took it there. Then you can **feel guilty / tell the truth** and **feel good / return** the jacket to your mom.

2. **Jim:** My mom asked me who took the money that was on the table. I told her my little brother took it. And now, he's going to **tell the truth / get in trouble** and I don't **feel guilty / feel good** about it.

   Sam: You should tell your mom the truth, you know? If you tell the truth, it'll be OK. And tell your brother that you're sorry. But who took the money?

   Jim: I don't know.

4 Read the dilemma. What do you think? Complete the sentences. Use the expressions in the box or your own ideas.

> You and your friend find an expensive jacket. There's a wallet with an address in it. Your friend takes the jacket to the owner. The owner gives your friend a reward of $50.00. Your friend keeps the money and doesn't say anything to you. Then you learn the truth.

be upset with	feel good	feel guilty	tell the truth

1. How do you feel?

   I _____.

2. How should your friend feel?

   My friend _____.

3. How do you think your friend feels?

   My friend probably _____.

4. What should your friend have done?

   My friend should have _____.

5. What should or shouldn't you do?

   _____

5 Listen and read. Circle the correct answer.

GARY'S DILEMMA

Gary was walking out of school when his best friend Ryan ran up to him. "We're good, right? If my mom calls you, you'll say it's true that I'm studying with you, right?" he whispered. Behind Ryan stood Max and a gang of boys Gary didn't want to know.

Gary nodded, trying to smile.

"Come on, Ryan, let's go, dude!" Max called.

"Just a sec!" Ryan said. He turned back to Gary. "Thanks, Gary. See you soon, OK?"

"Yeah, sure," said Gary, and he turned and headed home. He wondered how he got into this dilemma with Ryan. He should have said no in the first place.

"Hey, Gary! Wait up!" Gary turned and saw Pete running toward him.

"Hi, Pete," said Gary, without looking at Pete.

"What's up with you?" Pete said.

"Sorry," said Gary, "I'm just thinking about something."

"By the way," Pete said, "what's up with Ryan? What's he doing hanging out with that creep Max and those other guys? That gang's always getting in trouble!"

"I don't know, but he can do whatever he wants," shrugged Gary.

Pete grabbed Gary's shoulder. "I can't believe you said that! Ryan's our friend. If he's in trouble, we should help him."

Gary looked down, thinking, *If I tell, Ryan will think he can't trust me, and I might lose him as a friend. I don't want to be in trouble with the gang, either. But if I don't tell, something terrible might happen to Ryan.* Gary had to make a decision.

1. Ryan and Gary **are / aren't** going to study together.

2. Gary **is / isn't** going to tell a lie to Ryan's mom.

3. Max and his gang **are / aren't** friends of Gary's.

4. Pete thinks he and Gary **have to / don't have** to do something to help Ryan.

6 Answer the questions. Use your own ideas.

1. Why do kids join gangs? Why do you think Ryan joined the gang?

_____

2. What should Gary and Pete do?

_____

7 Listen and read. Then answer the questions.

Mom: <u>What's the matter</u>, Chris?

Chris: Nothing, Mom.

Mom: Did something happen at school today?

Chris: Well . . . yeah, but it's not important.

Mom: <u>Look</u>. If you don't tell me what's wrong, I can't help you. Tell me <u>what's going on</u>.

Chris: Well, a couple of boys at school are <u>being mean</u> to me.

Mom: They are? Did they hurt you?

Chris: No, it's nothing like that. They're just <u>calling me names</u> once in a while.

Mom: I'm glad you told me, Chris. Let's think about what you can do.

1. What is Chris's dilemma? _____

2. What does Chris's mom want him to do? _____

3. Why doesn't Chris want to talk to his mom about his problem? _____

   _____

8 Look at 7. Read the underlined expressions. Match and write the letter.

___ **1.** What's the matter?   **a.** They're unkind and cruel.

___ **2.** Look.   **b.** What's up?

___ **3.** They're mean.   **c.** Listen.

___ **4.** They call me names.   **d.** What's wrong?

___ **5.** What's going on?   **e.** They tease and insult me.

9 Answer the questions.

1. Why do you think the boys at school are being mean to Chris?

   _____

2. What will you say to someone if he or she calls you names?

   _____

Grammar

If he **pays attention** in class, he**'ll understand** the lesson.

If they don**'t study** for the math test, they **won't get** a good grade.

If you **tell** me the truth, I**'ll help** you.

I can't be late!

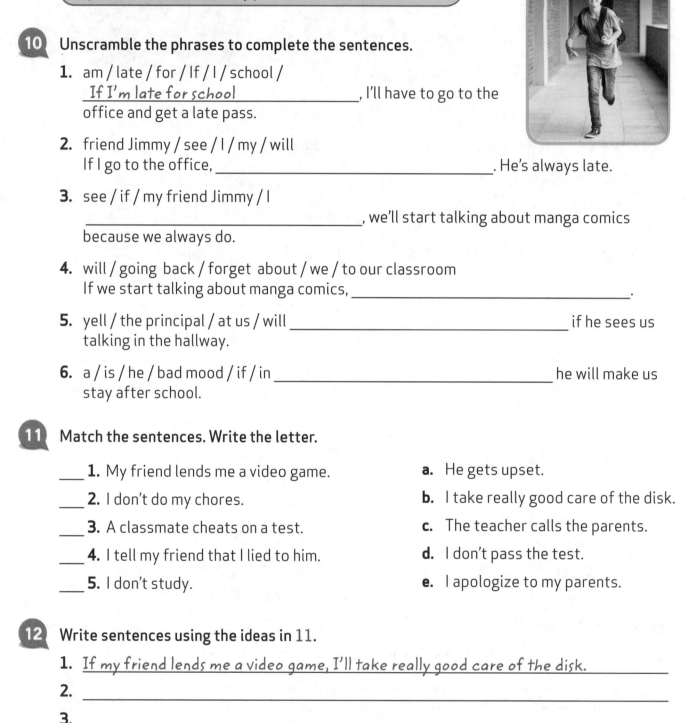

10 Unscramble the phrases to complete the sentences.

1. am / late / for / If / I / school /
   <u>If I'm late for school</u>, I'll have to go to the office and get a late pass.

2. friend Jimmy / see / I / my / will
   If I go to the office, _____. He's always late.

3. see / if / my friend Jimmy / I
   _____, we'll start talking about manga comics because we always do.

4. will / going back / forget about / we / to our classroom
   If we start talking about manga comics, _____.

5. yell / the principal / at us / will _____ if he sees us talking in the hallway.

6. a / is / he / bad mood / if / in _____ he will make us stay after school.

11 Match the sentences. Write the letter.

___ **1.** My friend lends me a video game.

___ **2.** I don't do my chores.

___ **3.** A classmate cheats on a test.

___ **4.** I tell my friend that I lied to him.

___ **5.** I don't study.

    a. He gets upset.

    b. I take really good care of the disk.

    c. The teacher calls the parents.

    d. I don't pass the test.

    e. I apologize to my parents.

12 Write sentences using the ideas in 11.

1. <u>If my friend lends me a video game, I'll take really good care of the disk.</u>

2. _____

3. _____

4. _____

5. _____

> You **should tell** your parents if you have a problem at school.
>
> If you don't want to get in trouble, you **shouldn't lie**.

13 **Read the advice column. Complete the sentences with the correct form of the words in the box. Add *should* if necessary.**

> call   find   give   say   start   stop   tell   tell

Ask Jenna and Jack: Smart Advice for Kids

Dear Jenna,

My friend keeps calling me names like "stupid" and "idiot." She always apologizes later, but it makes me upset. I told her to stop, but she doesn't. What should I do?

Sad Samantha

Dear Sad Samantha,

This girl is NOT your friend! If this girl _____ you names again, you _____ her to apologize immediately. If she _____ no, you _____ a new friend!

Jenna

Dear Jack,

My little brother is always following me around. I feel guilty when I tell him to stop, because he cries, but I don't want him hanging around. My friends don't like it either. What should I do?

Guilty Gordon

Dear Guilty Gordon,

This is a difficult problem. Arrange times to play with your little brother. Then tell him that he can't follow you with your friends. If he _____ to follow you and your friends, you _____ him to stop. Say that you and he will play together later. If he _____ following you, you _____ him a reward. Good luck!

Jack

14 **Complete the sentences with advice. Use *should* or *shouldn't*.**

1. If you borrow something from a friend, _____.

2. If someone is mean to you, _____.

3. If you have a problem at school, _____.

15 Listen and read. Then circle the correct answer to complete the sentences.

Ethics
1. Ethics is knowing what good and bad behavior is.
2. Your **character** is all of your traits and qualities taken together: such as being friendly, honest, and hard-working.
3. Treat means how you act toward others. Do you **treat** people nicely, or are you mean?
4. Ethical behavior is when you do the right thing and treat someone fairly and respectfully.

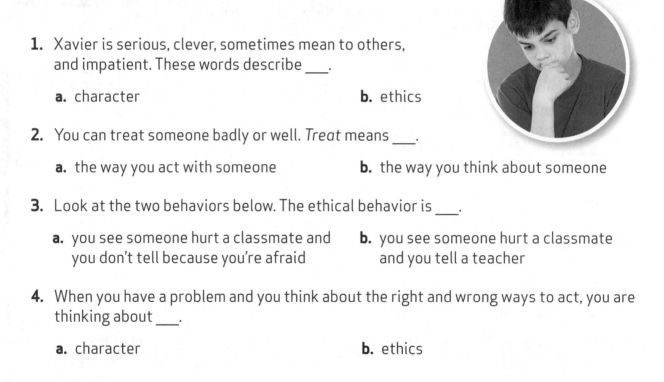

1. Xavier is serious, clever, sometimes mean to others, and impatient. These words describe ___.

   a. character   **b.** ethics

2. You can treat someone badly or well. *Treat* means ___.

   a. the way you act with someone   **b.** the way you think about someone

3. Look at the two behaviors below. The ethical behavior is ___.

   a. you see someone hurt a classmate and you don't tell because you're afraid   **b.** you see someone hurt a classmate and you tell a teacher

4. When you have a problem and you think about the right and wrong ways to act, you are thinking about ___.

   a. character   **b.** ethics

16 Match the proverbs to their meanings.

_____ **1.** "A clear conscience (mind) is a soft pillow."

_____ **2.** "Better to be alone than in bad company."

_____ **3.** "A friend's eye is a good mirror."

a. I don't need friends if they aren't good ones.

b. I trust my friends to tell me the truth about myself.

c. If I don't tell the truth, I won't feel good about myself (and might not be able to sleep at night).

17 Read. Match the stories to their proverbs above. Write 1, 2, or 3.

Proverbs From Around the World

Dilemma A: _____
Nellie is a new student at school. She's very shy, so she finds it hard to make friends. A group of girls asks Nellie if she wants to be friends. Nellie is very happy to say yes. She feels like she is part of a group and is happy because the girls are fun to be with. But Nellie begins to notice that these girls are loud in class and don't pay much attention to the teacher. The girls notice that Nellie is good in math. They ask her to do their math homework. They say if she doesn't, they'll tell lies about her. Nellie feels so hurt. She tells the girls that she won't be their friend. The girls tell lies about Nellie, but Nellie doesn't care. She walks alone to school and feels good about herself.

Dilemma B: _____
Doug hasn't been doing his homework. He has stopped hanging out with his friends. He just wants to make robots and listen to music. He keeps making promises to people, but he never keeps them. Today, he was supposed to help Calvin fix his bike, but he didn't. Calvin stops by Doug's house. He says that Doug is not acting like a friend. He's not being responsible. Calvin tells Doug that he should talk to his parents or to a counselor at school. Doug gets really angry and says that Calvin is crazy. Calvin leaves. Doug thinks about his behavior, and he admits that Calvin is probably right. Calvin's a good friend.

Dilemma C: _____
Gloria and Zelda are Tatiana's best friends. They told Tatiana that they stole some bracelets at the Art Fair last Saturday at school. Tatiana's teacher, Ms. Friedman, thought she saw Deanna near the bracelets, so now everyone thinks that Deanna took them. Tatiana doesn't know Deanna well, but she feels awful. Gloria and Zelda beg Tatiana not to tell anyone. They say they won't do it again. Tatiana can't stand the guilt. She decides to tell anyway. She feels good about the decision, but very sad for her friends. She hopes they understand and that they can stay friends. She knows they just made a stupid mistake.

18 Which proverb and story do you like best? Why?

_____

_____

Writing | Story Ending

A well-written story ends in a way that seems "right" or possible for the main character. Here are ways to help you decide what endings are "right" or possible:

- Find information in the story about the character's traits.
- Notice how the character treats others.
- Look at the character's actions and feelings.

19 Read *Gary's Dilemma* on page 24 again. Circle the traits that describe Gary's character.

> caring   funny   honest   lazy
> mean   not honest   serious   worried

20 Complete the sentences about Gary. Include one of the traits you circled in 19 and ideas from the story. Use the ideas in the box or your own ideas.

> asks his parents what he should do   says nothing and hopes that Ryan is okay
> talks to the gang members   tells a teacher about Ryan
> tells Ryan he should stop hanging around the gang   tells Ryan's parents

I think that Gary is _____ (trait) because in the story he _____

_____ .

It is possible that he will _____ .

I don't think that Gary will _____ .

21 Think about Gary's character. What does he do the next day? Answer the questions.

1. What is the first thing that he does? What happens to Gary and Ryan? Are they still friends? Why or why not?

_____

_____

_____

22 Write an ending to Gary's Dilemma on another piece of paper. Look at 19, 20, and 21 to help you. Begin: The next day, Gary made a decision.

23 Match the expressions and the situations. Write the letter.

___ **1.** tell the truth

___ **2.** feel guilty

___ **3.** cheat

___ **4.** feel good

___ **5.** get in trouble

___ **6.** be upset with

a. Amy looked at Suzie's test and copied the answers.

b. Steve's teacher is mad at him because he didn't do his homework.

c. Meg feels bad because she hurt Evan's feelings.

d. Manuel hit Ryan on the playground, and he had to go to the principal's office.

e. Jeff said that Claire took the money. She did.

f. Monica helped Robert study for his test. She is happy she could help him.

24 Tell what will happen. Use *will* and the words in parentheses.

1. Maya found out her brother cheated on a test. She wants to <u>tell her parents</u>. What will her brother do? (be / angry)

   <u>If Maya tells her parents, her brother will be very upset with her.</u>

2. Janet stole some money from her mom. She wants to <u>apologize to her mom</u>. What will her mom do? (say / disappointed)

   _____

3. Zena got into trouble because she was with a group of girls who called a young boy names and made him cry. She wants to <u>apologize</u>. What will he probably do? (say / OK)

   _____

1 Unscramble the words. Complete the phrases.

SCHOOL ACTIVITIES

1. turn in an _____
2. do _____
3. study for a _____ test _____
4. pay _____
5. be _____

ttse	test
_____	atttionen
hmwokroe	_____
_____	atmssgnine
cfulare	_____

_____   saekp

pbishlu   _____

_____   cblmi

boemec   _____

_____   wni

REACHING GOALS

1. _____ a book
2. _____ a doctor
3. _____ 2 languages
4. _____ a tournament
5. _____ a mountain

MAKING CHOICES

1. _____ on a test
2. _____ guilty
3. be _____
4. _____ the truth
5. get in _____

tspeu	_____
_____	toruble
fele	_____
_____	eltl
cetah	_____

2 **Find a song that makes you think about school days, goals, or dilemmas. Complete the chart.**

Song Title _____

Singer's or Group's Name _____

What language is used in the song? _____

How long have you liked this singer? _____

How long has this singer been performing? _____

What is the song about? _____

What happens in the song? _____

_____

If you can change words (lyrics) in the _____

song, what lyrics will you change? _____

_____

3 **Draw pictures to illustrate your song. Then write the story of your song on a separate piece of paper.**

4 **In Your Classroom**

Work in pairs and share.

unit 4 DREAMS FOR THE FUTURE

1 Match the pictures to the predictions. Check (✓) when you think the predictions may come true.

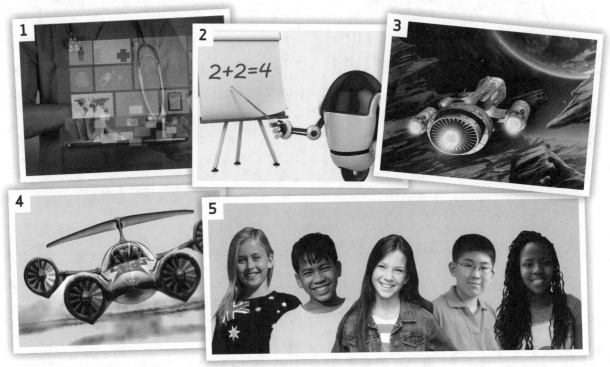

Predictions for the Future	Now	In My Lifetime	Never
___ Spaceships to other planets will depart daily.			
___ Robots will be teaching in the classroom.			
___ People around the world will be living happily together.			
___ We will be driving flying cars.			
___ We will be making progress in finding cures for many serious diseases.			

2 Look at 1. Explain one of your predictions.

_____

_____

3 Match each picture with a phrase.

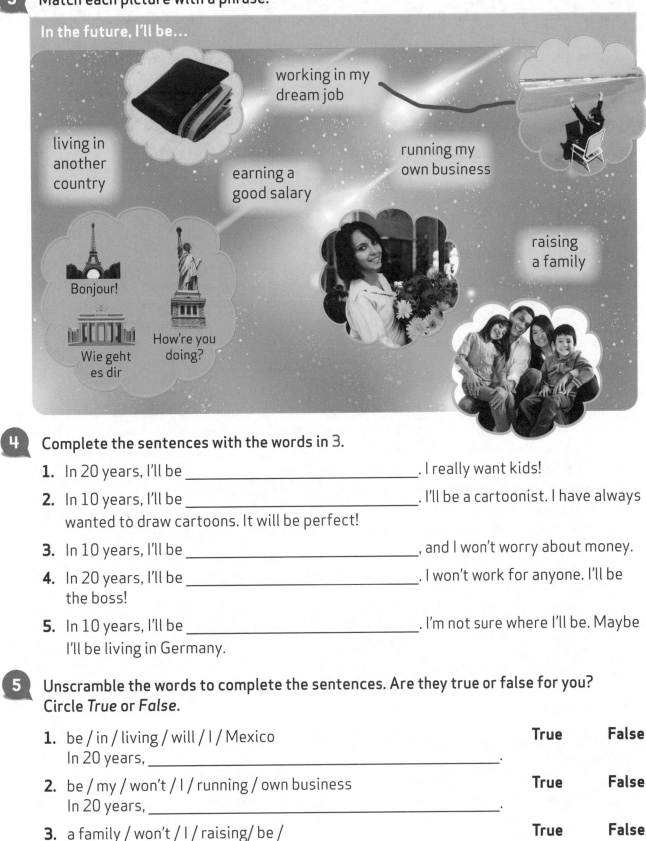

In the future, I'll be...

working in my dream job

living in another country

earning a good salary

running my own business

raising a family

Bonjour!

Wie geht es dir

How're you doing?

4 Complete the sentences with the words in 3.

1. In 20 years, I'll be _____. I really want kids!

2. In 10 years, I'll be _____. I'll be a cartoonist. I have always wanted to draw cartoons. It will be perfect!

3. In 10 years, I'll be _____, and I won't worry about money.

4. In 20 years, I'll be _____. I won't work for anyone. I'll be the boss!

5. In 10 years, I'll be _____. I'm not sure where I'll be. Maybe I'll be living in Germany.

5 Unscramble the words to complete the sentences. Are they true or false for you? Circle *True* or *False*.

1. be / in / living / will / I / Mexico
   In 20 years, _____.   **True**   **False**

2. be / my / won't / I / running / own business
   In 20 years, _____.   **True**   **False**

3. a family / won't / I / raising/ be /
   In 10 years, _____.   **True**   **False**

4. a good / earning / will / I / salary / be
   In 10 years, _____.   **True**   **False**

6 Listen and read the email. Then check (✓) the predictions Christina makes about her classmates.

TO	classmatesall@school.org
CC	
SUBJECT	Christina's Predictions

Dear Sixth Graders,

As class president, it's my job to think about your experiences as sixth graders. But I've been thinking a lot about my future lately, and since you know how curious and nosey I am, I can't help but think about your futures, too. It's never too early to think about what we'll be doing in 10 or 20 years. I thought it would be fun to start the conversation. This is what I predict:

I'll start with me. I know that in 10 years I'll be running my own business in the fashion industry. That doesn't surprise you, does it? You know how I love fashion, and I love to be the boss. One thing I won't be doing is living in this city! I want to live abroad—maybe in Tokyo or Paris. I think Jessie will be working in his dream job as a cartoonist because that's all I see him doing in school. I bet he will be making animation films. In 10 years, Stephanie will definitely be working in the music industry. She's got an awesome voice. Don't you agree? George will be taking adventurous trips abroad because he'll be a famous journalist. He's so smart and he works so hard. I hope that all of these predictions come true!

That's not all, but that's all I have time for now. If you want to reply, let me know your dreams, and I'll add them to this school blog. Let's all think about our dreams and reach for the stars this year!

Your Class President,

Christina

Predictions

☐ **1.** working in his dream job   ☐ **5.** living in this city
☐ **2.** working in the music industry   ☐ **6.** speaking foreign languages
☐ **3.** earning a good salary   ☐ **7.** married
☐ **4.** famous   ☐ **8.** taking adventurous trips

7 Make a prediction about what you will be doing in 20 years and explain why.

I will be _____ because _____.

8 Listen and read. Then circle the answers.

Brandon: What do you think you'll be doing after you graduate from high school, Serena?

Serena: College, I'm sure. How about you? What will you be doing in, say, fifteen years?

Brandon: I'll be working on a big movie!

Serena: A movie? You think you'll be a movie star after you graduate?

Brandon: No, not a movie star. A movie director. I'll be working with all the big Hollywood stars.

Serena: Really? And how will you do that?

Brandon: Well, I'm pretty good at making short movies on my computer right now. I just need one big break, and *voilà*! I'll be the next Spielberg!

Serena: Sure. I just hope you won't forget us once you're rich and famous!

Brandon: Of course not! Mom and you will be walking on the red carpet with me!

Serena: Oh, I like that idea!

1. What does Brandon think he'll be doing in 15 years?

    a. He'll be acting in movies.   **b.** He'll be directing movies.   **c.** He'll be in college.

2. Young actors and singers are always looking for a big break in their career. What does *a big break* mean?

    a. a big rest   **b.** a chance to be successful   **c.** a chance to travel

3. When an actor is *on the red carpet*, what is he or she invited to attend?

    a. the Oscar awards ceremony   **b.** college   **c.** a reading of the movie script

4. The word *voilá* is French. People say "voilá" when they show or tell you something surprising. What is the surprise that comes after Brandon's big break?

    a. He'll meet Steven Spielberg.   **b.** He'll be a famous director like Steven Spielberg.   **c.** He'll be speaking French to everyone.

9 Read the dialogue in **8** again. Does Brandon think he'll be successful? Why or why not?

_____

_____

_____

Grammar

What **will** you **be doing** ten years from now?	I'll definitely **be studying** at a big university in the city.
Where **will** you **be living** in twenty years?	I probably **won't be living** in Europe.

10 Match. Then answer the questions. Use the future progressive form of the verbs and *definitely* or *probably*.

Hopes and Dreams in 20 years

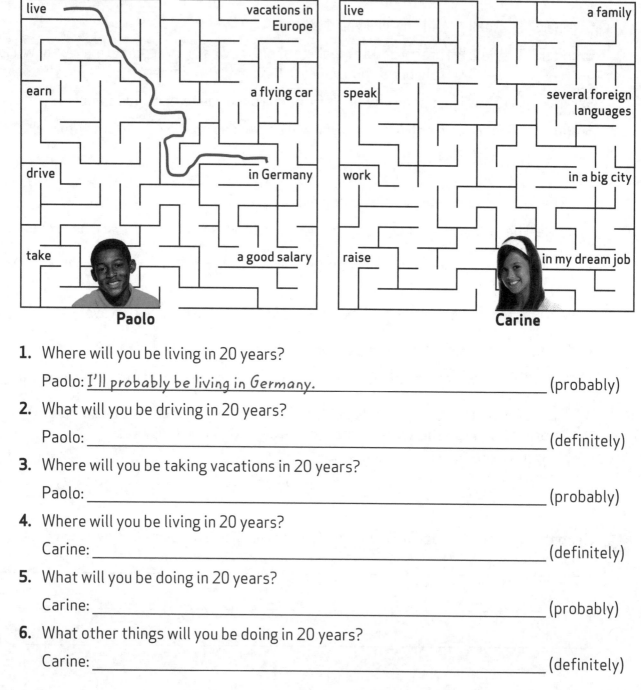

Paolo

Carine

1. Where will you be living in 20 years?

   Paolo: <u>I'll probably be living in Germany.</u> _____ (probably)

2. What will you be driving in 20 years?

   Paolo: _____ (definitely)

3. Where will you be taking vacations in 20 years?

   Paolo: _____ (probably)

4. Where will you be living in 20 years?

   Carine: _____ (definitely)

5. What will you be doing in 20 years?

   Carine: _____ (probably)

6. What other things will you be doing in 20 years?

   Carine: _____ (definitely)

Will you **be running** a business?	No, definitely not. I definitely won't . . . Yes, definitely. I definitely will . . . Probably not. I probably won't . . . Yes, probably. I probably will . . .

11 **Answer the questions. Use the information in 10.**

1. Will Carine be working in her dream job in 20 years?

   _____

2. Will Paolo be living in Germany in 20 years?

   _____

3. Will Carine be living in a small city in 20 years?

   _____

4. Will Paolo be taking vacations in Asia?

   _____

5. Will Carine be raising a family in 20 years?

   _____

6. Will Paolo be driving a flying car in 20 years?

   _____

12 **Answer the questions about your future life in college with**
No, definitely not, Yes, definitely, **or** *Probably not.*

1. Will you be seeing your family a lot when you go
   to college?

   _____

2. Will you be studying a foreign language in college?

   _____

3. Will you be studying harder than you do now?

   _____

13 **Choose a friend. Write a question about your friend's future in college. Ask your friend the**
questions. Then write the answer *No, definitely not, Yes, definitely,* **or** *Probably not.*

Q: _____

A: _____

14 Listen and read.

Two Trends in Medicine

There are two important trends in the future of medicine. One is nanotechnology. The word *nano* means billionth. That's really tiny! Scientists who are working in nanotechnology are studying particles that are so small that they are invisible to the human eye! In fact, they have to measure these particles with a new unit of measurement, called the nanometer. Do you see the word "meter" in nanometer? You know how long a meter is, right? For example, a baseball bat is about a meter long. Can you imagine something that is only 1/1,000,000,000 of a baseball bat?! One example of this is the nanorobot. These microscopic robots are made of the same material that we are made of: DNA. In the future scientists will be using nanorobots to treat diseases and illnesses. For example, when you become sick in the future, doctors will put a nanorobot into your body. The robot will find the cause of your illness and give the correct medicine to help it heal. Wouldn't that be great?! Think of it: When you become sick, your insides will be like a video game: robots will be searching for "the bad guys" and destroying them!

The second trend is in virtual medicine. Thirty years from now, when you have a fever and are feeling sick, you will not have to leave your home and go to a doctor. You will be using wireless technology in your own home to diagnose and treat your illness. In this futuristic scenario, you will take 3D pictures of your body using an object like a TV remote control. You will upload these images to a website. The doctor will download these images and review them and upload medicine for you to download. If the doctor wants to talk to you, the doctor will talk with you through a video call – or maybe he or she will "visit" you virtually using 3D technology. The doctor will look like he or she is in your room, but it will just be a 3D image. Wouldn't that be cool?

15 Think about the size of things around you. The head of a pin is 2,000,000 (2 million) nanometers wide. What is the size of these objects in nanometers? Guess and circle.

1. An ant is about ___ nanometers (nm) wide.
   - **a.** 5,000
   - **b.** 50,000
   - **c.** 5,000,000

2. A human hair is about ___ nanometers (nm) wide.
   - **a.** 12,000
   - **b.** 120,000
   - **c.** 1,200,000

3. A man who is 6 feet 5 inches tall is ___ nanometers (nm) tall.
   - **a.** 2 million
   - **b.** 2 billion
   - **c.** 2 trillion

16 Read. Then answer the questions.

Young Inventors

What will your future look like? It depends on the inventions that inventors are dreaming up today, right? And who are those inventors? You might think that inventors are old people who have worked for many years on their ideas. That may have been what inventors looked like years ago, but in this technological age, that view of inventors is disappearing.

Researchers today think the ideas for inventions will come from children. They recently interviewed young kids, ages 12 and under, from all around the world and asked them what they thought computers would be like in the future. They were amazed by how many wonderful and inventive ideas the kids told them. These kids were very comfortable with technology and they wanted to see computers do more and more for them. In fact, the kids wanted computers to look and act human. They didn't think it would be strange to have a computer as a friend! They did have some differences of opinion about what exactly they wanted computers to do. Some kids said they wanted computers that would play with them and help them with homework. Other kids wanted to use computers to learn new skills and do things more easily, like speaking a foreign language. Others wanted to use computers to create things, like video games and virtual-reality places.

Everyone thought it would be great if they could mix online and real-life experiences. For example, they wanted to be able to see things online—like a sandwich—and make it into a real sandwich using a machine like a printer. Sounds cool, doesn't it?

What do you think of these ideas? Do you agree that kids like you will be creating new inventions for the future? Maybe you have an idea for an invention. If you do, draw it, write about it, and tell someone! You may be the next Steve Jobs!

17 Answer the questions.

1. Do you think kids are better than adults at thinking up new ideas with computers? Why or why not?

_____

_____

2. The kids had different ideas about computers. What do you want computers to do?

_____

_____

3. Kids liked the idea of seeing something on the computer, like a sandwich, and making it real using a machine. What would you like to make real?

_____

_____

When you write an email, you need to think about who you are writing to. If you are writing to a teacher or other adult, you will write a formal email. If you are writing to a friend, you will write an informal email. Here are some ways these two kinds of emails are different.

	Formal Email	Informal Email
1. **Subject**	1. Be clear and specific. *This week's writing assignment.*	1. Write something simple. *Tonight* or *Hi.*
2. **Greeting**	2. Use Ms. / Mr. / Mrs. *Mrs. Sanchez.*	2. Write *Hi Tony,* or *Hey Tony,*
3. **Body**	3. Write your message in full sentences, check your spelling, and be polite. *I missed class yesterday because I was sick. Can I get my homework assignments, please?*	3. u can use short words cuz u wanna write quickly to ur bff.
4. **Closing**	4. Write *Sincerely,* or *Best,* and your name below.	4. Write your name.

18 Read each sentence. Write *formal* if it belongs in a formal email or *informal* if it belongs in an informal email. Add commas where necessary.

1. _____ Hey Tami,

2. _____ I am having trouble deciding what to do for my science project. Could you help me with some ideas?

3. _____ c u later bff!

4. _____ Dear Mr. Taylor,

5. _____ Sincerely, Xavier

19 Write a formal and informal email on a separate piece of paper. In the informal email, use abbreviations from the Texting Abbreviations box.

Tips

Texting Abbreviations

b4 = before

bff = best friends forever

c = see

cuz = because

gonna = going to

TTYL = talk to you later

u = you

wanna = want to

Vocabulary and Grammar | Review

20 Complete the sentences. Use the future progressive of the verbs in parentheses.

Carlos and his sister Bianca have big plans for the future. Carlos _____
(1)
probably _____ (go) to college in ten years. Once he graduates, he
(2)
_____ (work) as a businessman with his dad. He _____ definitely
(3)
_____ (live) in another country because he wants to stay close to his family in
(4)
Mexico City.

Bianca _____ probably _____ (start) her
(5)
studies in chemistry. She has always wanted to be a scientist. In 20
years, she _____ definitely _____ (earn) a
(6)
good salary. She _____ probably _____ (live) in
(7)
Mexico because she has always wanted to travel in foreign countries.

Both Carlos and Bianca _____ (raise) big families. They both want to have
(8)
lots of children.

21 Choose a family member. Complete the sentences about that family member's future
using the future progressive. Use *will* or *won't* and the words from the box or your
own words.

| dream job | earning a good salary | famous |
| married | running his or her own business | taking adventurous vacations |

1. My family member's name is _____ .
2. This person _____ in 10 years.
3. This person _____ in 20 years.

22 Answer the questions. Use *Yes, definitely, Yes, probably, No, probably not,* or *No,
definitely not.*

1. In your lifetime, do you think you will be working with intelligent beings from outer space?

_____

2. Do you think people will be living on other planets in the next century?

_____

unit 5 IF I COULD FLY...

1 Which superpowers do these characters have? Match the characters with their superpower. Write the number.

___ able to climb tall buildings   ___ is super strong

___ runs faster than the wind   ___ disappears with the snap of a finger

___ saves the world from bad guys   ___ travels through time and space

2 Answer the questions.

1. What superpower would make your life better?

_____

2. How would the superpower improve your life?

_____

3. Who are your favorite superheroes or superheroines? What powers do they have?

_____

3 Match the beginning of the phrases to their endings. Then match the phrases to the pictures. Write the number under the picture.

Now you see me!

It's easy!

Now you don't!

A ___   B ___   C ___   D ___

___ **1.** run at
___ **2.** travel
___ **3.** have
___ **4.** become

a. invisible
b. super human strength
c. lightning speed
d. through time

4 Complete the sentences with the phrases in 3.

1. I want to meet people who lived long ago. If I could have a superpower,

I would _____.

2. I want to go places without people being able to see me. If I could have a superpower,

I would _____.

3. I want to be able to get anywhere in a few seconds! If I could have a superpower,

I would _____.

4. I want to be really strong so that I can pick up anything I want! If I could

have a superpower, I would _____.

5 Complete the sentences. If you had these superpowers, what would you do? Use the ideas in the box or your own ideas.

> go and visit family members who lived a long time ago
>
> save people in fires and other dangerous situations
>
> move my home to different places during summer vacations
>
> tell people when someone is lying to them

1. If I could have super strength, I would _____.

2. If I could read minds, I would _____.

3. If I could travel through time, I would _____.

Reading | Graphic Novel

6 Listen and read. Then circle *True* or *False*.

1. Bulldog and Power Paws know each other.   True   False
2. Bulldog is happy to see Power Paws.   True   False
3. Bulldog isn't scared of Power Paws.   True   False
4. Bulldog knows that Power Paws is going to make him small. True   False
5. Power Paws has special powers.   True   False

7 Answer the questions.

1. What is Bulldog doing to Duck?

   _____

2. Why is Power Paws going to make Bulldog small?

   _____

3. Do you think Duck will take good care of Bulldog?

   _____

8 Listen and read. Then circle the correct answers.

Girl: Dad, do you think we'll ever be able to travel through time?

Dad: Wow, <u>that's a hard one</u>. A lot is possible today, but I really don't see how time travel would be possible. Do you think so?

Girl: I'm not sure, but it would be fun if we could! If you could <u>go back in time</u>, where would you go?

Dad: Hmm. <u>Let me think</u> ... Maybe I'd go back to see my great-grandparents who lived in London. My great-grandfather was a shoemaker there—did I ever tell you that? I'm told he was <u>quite a character</u>. I would love to talk to him. What would you do?

Girl: Me? Oh, I know already—that's easy. If I could travel through time, I'd go back to last night and study more. I don't feel ready for my test this afternoon.

1. The dad thinks the girl's question is ___ to answer.

   a. easy   **b.** not easy

2. The girl ___ travel back in time.

   a. wants to   **b.** doesn't want to

3. The girl ___ stories about her great-grandfather.

   a. has heard   **b.** hasn't heard

4. The girl ___ hard for her math test.

   a. studied   **b.** didn't study

9 Match the phrases to their meanings.

___ **1.** That's a hard one.

___ **2.** go back in time

___ **3.** quite a character

___ **4.** Let me think.

   a. It means "to travel to a time in the past."

   b. It means "a funny, interesting, unique person" that people like.

   c. It means "I need a little time to think of an answer." It's similar to "That's a hard one."

   d. It means "That's a difficult question." You say this when the question isn't easy to answer. It's similar to "Let me think."

10 Complete the sentence. Use a phrase from 9.

The teacher asks you, "Who is your favorite superhero?" You need to think about your answer, so you say _____ .

Grammar

if clause	result clause
If I **were** you,	I'**d choose** something else.
If he **made** his bed every day,	his mother **would be** happy.
If she **could have** one superpower,	she'**d breathe** under water.

11 Complete the sentences with the words given.

1. (would, study, were) If I _____ you,
   I _____ harder. You would get better grades.

2. (could, would, fly, visit) If she _____ ,
   she _____ her aunt and uncle in California all the time.

3. (could, would, run, win) If the track team _____ at lightning
   speed, it _____ all its tournaments.

4. (would, be, did) If all the students _____ their homework all
   the time, the teacher _____ happy.

5. (could, would, know, read) If I _____ my teacher's mind,
   I _____ the answers to all her questions.

12 Read. Complete the sentences with the words given. Use *could* and *would*.

I can't sing well. But if I _____
(sing) well, I _____ (join) a band.

My friends and I can't travel back in time. If
we _____ (travel) back in time,
we _____ (meet) our favorite
heroes in history.

My older brother can't drive yet. If he
_____ (drive), he
_____ (take) my friends
and me to the movies.

My friend can't be quiet in class. If she
_____ (be) quiet, our
teacher _____ (be) happier.

13 Complete the sentences about yourself.

1. If I could meet a famous person, I _____.

2. _____, I would be very happy.

48 Unit 5

| If you **didn't have to go** to school, what **would** you **do** every day? | If I **didn't have to go** to school, I **would stay** home and **listen** to music all day. |
| If you **could go** anywhere, where **would** you **go**? | If I **could go** anywhere, I'**d go** to Vera Cruz. |

14 Complete the questions. Unscramble the words.

(you / would / go / where)

1. If you could visit any country you wanted to, _____?

(would / which language / you / study)

2. If you could study another language (not English), _____?

(you / be / would / which animal)

3. If you could be any animal, _____?

(be / who / you / would)

4. If you could be any superhero, _____?

(would / play / what / you)

5. If you could play any instrument, _____?

15 Match the questions in 14 to the answers below. Write the numbers. Then circle *True* or *False*.

___ **1.** I would be a wolf because wolves are really smart animals.　　　**True**　　**False**

___ **2.** I would visit Italy to see the art.　　　**True**　　**False**

___ **3.** I would study Chinese.　　　**True**　　**False**

___ **4.** I would be Spider-Man because I think it would be fun to climb walls.　**True**　**False**

___ **5.** I would play the piano.　　　**True**　　**False**

16 Ask the questions in 14 to a friend or family member. Write his or her answers.

1. _____

2. _____

3. _____

4. _____

Listen and read. Then answer the questions.

Superpower or Invention?

Some researchers have developed products that seem to give us superpower-like abilities. One of these inventions is the super sticky adhesive that they created by studying geckos and their sticky feet. Another invention is the ability to tell a computer what to do with our minds. A third invention is our ability to visualize a computer anywhere we want one—even on our hands. Let's think about what our lives might be like if we had these products today.

In the morning, you wake up. Your bed is stuck on the wall, so you walk down a ladder to get to the floor. There is space under your bed now to hang out with friends, so you like that. After breakfast, you put on your super sticky shoes and hand pads. On your way to school, you climb up the wall to a window where your friend Timmy lives. He sees you. You both climb down the wall and start walking to school.

"Oh no!" you suddenly say, "I forgot my homework!" You think, *Mom, please send my math homework to school.* Your mom gets the message on her smartphone and texts back, "OK." You think, *Thanks, Mom!* Your mind is connected to your computer at home, so you can send messages to it or to your parents' smartphones. Then, your friend says, "I wonder what the reviews are for the new superhero movie?" He draws a box on your backpack and a computer appears. He goes to a movie review website and reads the latest reviews to you as you walk.

At school, you climb up the wall and hang your jacket on a hook. Your teacher gives you a quiz and tells you, "Don't draw computers anywhere. If you studied, you will know every answer." You didn't study much, so you're thinking, *If I could see the book in my mind, I could look up the answers.* Researchers haven't figured out how to give you perfect memory—but they are probably working on it.

1. Where did the idea of a sticky adhesive come from?

   _____

2. "To develop something" means it took a long time to make something work well. Which invention do you think would take the longest to create? Why?

   _____

3. Do you think it would be fun to walk up walls? If so, why?

   _____

4. Pretend that you can draw computers anywhere and use them. Where would you use them? What would you do?

   _____

18 Read. Then read and write the names of the superheroes.

Superheros from Around the World

Superheroes from around the world each have unique abilities to protect people and destroy evil.

Cat Girl Nuku Nuku is from Japan. She is a student, but when something terrible happens, she becomes a superhero! She can react quickly when something bad happens, just like a cat. She can smell, see, and hear very well because she has the senses of a cat. She also has superhuman strength.

Meteroix is from Mexico. He is a student and his everyday name is Aldo. He has superhuman strength and can throw bolts of lightning. When he has to protect himself, he covers himself with blue armor by swallowing a meteorite.

Darna is from the Philippines. Her everyday name is Narda and she is a student. Darna can fly and has superhuman strength and speed. She cannot be destroyed by weapons that humans make. She can change back and forth between her two identities by swallowing a stone and shouting the name of her other identity.

Superheroes are fun to read about, but do you sometimes wish that they were real? If these superheroes were real, they would have many things to do every day!

1. Human weapons cannot destroy this superhero. _____

2. Bolts of lightning are weapons of this superhero. _____

3. This superhero acts like a cat. _____

19 Read. Which superhero can help? Why?

1. Some bank robbers are coming out of a bank. They have a very big weapon. They are running away! Who can help? Why?

   _____

2. An evil person from space wants to steal all the gold and diamonds in the world. It is hard to find her because she is very tiny and can hide very easily. She loves peanut butter and always has peanut butter cookies in her pockets.

   _____

3. Some bad guys have thousands of fighters helping them. The bad guys want to destroy the government. The bad guys are attacking now!

   _____

When you write a description of a character, tell everything about that character:

1. name(s)
2. occupation
3. country of origin
4. time period that he or she lives in: now, the future, the past
5. appearance
6. superpowers
7. family
8. mission

20 Read the sentences and match them to the information in the box. Write the numbers. Be careful! What information is missing? Write the numbers.

___ Her everyday name is Diana, but her superhero name is Wonder Woman.

___ She has super strength, and she is an excellent fighter. She has a rope that makes people tell the truth and an invisible jet.

___ She is from a place near Greece in ancient times.

___ She has many sisters.

Missing information: Numbers ___ ___ ___ ___

21 Read the missing information from **20** below. Number it according to the information in the writing box.

___ lived in the past, and lives in the present, too	___ make villains honest
___ in many stories she is an officer in the U.S. army	___ is tall / has long dark hair

22 Write a description of Wonder Woman. Use the information in **20** and **21**.

_____

_____

_____

_____

_____

_____

23 Match the phrases to make sentences. Write the letter.

___ **1.** If I could read people's minds,

___ **2.** If I could run at lightning speed,

___ **3.** If I could travel through time,

___ **4.** If I could fly,

a. I'd be faster than a jet plane.

b. I'd know what they were thinking.

c. I'd go back and play with my grandpa when he was young.

d. I'd take my sisters and brothers for rides in the sky with me.

24 Complete the sentences with your own ideas.

1. If _____ , I'd know why you are upset with me.

2. If _____ , I'd move your house closer to mine. Then I could see you more often.

3. If I could invent something to help other people, _____ .

4. If I _____ , my family would be very happy.

25 Read. Circle the correct answers.

1. If people ___ wings, they wouldn't drive cars.

  a. have   **b.** had

2. If she had enough money, she ___ those earrings. But she doesn't have enough money.

  a. 'd buy   **b.** buys

3. You're really smart. If I ___ you, I'd try out for a TV game show.

  a. were   **b.** be

4. If my older brother went to bed earlier, he ___ so tired every morning.

  a. is not going to be   **b.** would not be

26 Answer the questions with your own ideas.

1. If you found 20 dollars, what would you do with the money?

_____

2. If you wrote a book, what would you write about?

_____

3. If you were a movie, what movie would you be?

_____

unit 6 THE COOLEST SCHOOL SUBJECTS

1 Which school subjects do the pictures show? Write the number.

___ geography

___ art history

___ science

___ music

___ literature

___ world history

___ P.E.

___ math

2 If you could choose three subjects to add to your school year, what would they be? Check your answer or add your own ideas.

- ☐ computer science
- ☐ Spanish language
- ☐ orchestra
- ☐ theatre
- ☐ _____

- ☐ government
- ☐ chemistry
- ☐ tennis
- ☐ ecosystems and ecology
- ☐ _____

3 **Unscramble the words. Use the words to complete the sentences.**

1. MYCROEACD DEMOCRACY

   The word DEMOCRACY comes from a Greek word that means "power of the people." One of the first Western examples of this form of government was in Athens, in the 5th Century B.C.

2. MAMLAM _____

   The cheetah is the fastest _____ in the world. It can run about 100 meters in six seconds!

3. PTNAL _____

   The bladderwort is the deadliest meat-eating _____. It can kill a bug in less than a millisecond.

4. GIYRHWALTPS _____

   Shakespeare is one of the most famous _____ in English literature. He wrote approximately 40 plays in his lifetime, including comedies, tragedies, and historical plays.

5. PERMI BEURNM _____ _____

   The number 8 can be divided by 1 and 8, but it can also be divided by 2 and 4. As a result, it is not a _____ _____.

6. RTSATI _____

   Georgia O'Keefe is a famous American _____. She is famous for her amazing paintings of flowers.

4 **Match these sentences with the class. Write the letters.**

___ 1. I want to learn more about myths and legends.

___ 2. I love reading about democracies all over the world.

___ 3. We have a grammar test today.

___ 4. In today's class, we learned that blue whales are the largest mammals in the world!

___ 5. We're painting a mural in class today.

___ 6. I love playing soccer!

a. P.E.

b. English

c. literature

d. art

e. social studies

f. science (biology)

5 Listen and read. Then answer the questions.

The Story of Daedalus and Icarus

Once upon a time, on the island of Crete, there was a man named Daedalus and his young son Icarus. They lived in the palace of King Minos. Daedalus was the smartest man in the palace. He was also one of the greatest inventors and architects of that time. He invented many things for the king, including an enormous type of maze, called The Labyrinth. King Minos did not want Daedalus to share the secrets of The Labyrinth with anyone. So he put Daedalus and Icarus in prison. Daedalus was very unhappy. He had only one wish. He wanted to be free.

One day, Daedalus was watching the birds fly. He admired their beautiful, strong wings. Watching the birds gave him an idea. If he created wings for Icarus and himself, they could fly away and be free! So Daedalus created wings of feathers and wax, and they put them on. Daedalus told Icarus, "Be careful! Don't fly too close to the water or you might fall into it! Don't fly too close to the sun, or the wax will melt and you will fall!" Icarus said that he would obey his father, but when they started flying, Icarus became extremely excited. He flew in circles and went higher and higher. He loved the feeling of freedom and flying. His father called out to him, "Come back here! Don't go so close to the sun!" Icarus wanted to listen, but the feeling of freedom was the best feeling in the world, so he kept flying higher. The sun became hotter and hotter and began to melt the wax. Icarus started to fly lower, but it was too late. Icarus's wings fell off, and he fell into the sea.

1. Why did King Minos keep Daedalus and Icarus in prison?

_____

2. Why did Daedalus want to escape?

_____

3. Why did Icarus fly higher and higher?

_____

4. What do you learn from this story?

_____

5. The Icarian Sea was named after Icarus. Do you know other places named after famous myths and legends? Write the names.

_____

6 Listen and read. Then circle the correct answer.

Julie: I haven't studied for the math test yet, have you?

Leo: Not yet. Hey, <u>let's form a study group</u>!

Julie: That's the smartest idea you've had in a long time!

Leo: Ha! Ha! Very funny.

379 009

Cathy: Great idea! The only thing I remember about prime numbers is that they're larger than 1.

Julie: <u>Speaking of</u> prime numbers, do you know the most amazing thing about the numbers 379009? Type them on a calculator and read them upside down. They spell GOOGLE.

Leo: <u>Seriously</u>? <u>Let me see</u> ... You're right! That's the coolest thing ever!

1. Why are the students going to get together?

   a. They're going to have fun.   **b.** They're going to study.

2. Does Cathy understand what prime numbers are?

   a. Yes   **b.** No

3. Why is 379009 an amazing number?

   a. It spells the word "GOOGLE" with numbers.   **b.** It's the largest prime number.

7 Look at 6. Read the underlined expressions. How can you say them in other words? Match the expressions with the sentences. Write the letters.

___ **1.** Let's form a study group.

___ **2.** Speaking of ...

___ **3.** Let me see.

___ **4.** Seriously?

a. By the way, that reminds me of something.

b. Really? I'm surprised.

c. Why don't we study together?

d. I want to try.

8 Complete the sentences with the expressions in 7. Then listen and check your answers.

A: I was just chosen to be on a TV game show.

B: ¹_____? Congratulations!

01134

A: Yeah, they asked me what happens when you turn 01134 upside down. I said it spells "hello."

B: ²_____. Wow! You're right!

A: ³_____ of numbers, ⁴_____ for the math test tomorrow.

B: Good idea!

China has **more** speakers of English **than** the U.S.

I have **fewer** school subjects **than** my brother.

Teachers in Finland give **less homework than** teachers in the U.S.

9 Complete these facts about countries. Circle *more*, *fewer*, or *less*.

1. People in Germany spend 18 hours a week watching TV. People in the United States spend 21 hours. People in the United States spend **less / more** time watching TV than people in Germany.

2. According to the World Atlas, Europe has 47 countries and Asia has 44 countries. There are **more / less** countries in Europe than in Asia.

3. In Mexico, there are approximately 55,000,000 males and 57,000,000 females. There are **less / fewer** males than females.

4. In Africa, people speak more than 2,000 languages. In North and South America, people speak almost 1,000 languages. People in Africa speak **more / less** languages than people in North and South America.

5. In Mexico, the dog is a **more / less** popular pet than a parakeet. People like parakeets better than dogs.

6. In India, 946 films are made per year. In the United States, 611 films are made per year. The United States makes **more / fewer** films per year than India.

10 Answer the questions. Write complete sentences.

1. Do you watch more or fewer hours of TV a week than people in the United States?

_____

2. In your country, is a rabbit a more popular pet than a cat?

_____

3. Do you think your country makes fewer or more films a year than the United States?

_____

4. Do you think your country has more or less people than the United States?

_____

5. In your class, are there more females or males?

_____

> The Amazon rain forest has **the most** species of plants and animals on earth.
>
> Germany and Switzerland have **the fewest** pet dogs per capita.
>
> Which country has **the least** amount of air pollution?

11 **Draw lines to connect the sentence parts.**

1. A tree in Nevada, in the U.S., is 4,800 years old. It is

2. Mexico City has more than 20 million tourists each year. It has

3. The kakapo parrot weighs 3.5 kilograms. It is

4. It rarely rains in the Atacama Desert in Chile. It has

5. Siberia has a very long railway. It has

6. The bumblebee bat only weighs two grams. It is

the least   tourists of any city in Mexico.

the longest   mammal in the world.

the oldest   amount of rain a year of all deserts.

the lightest   parrot in the world.

the heaviest   railway in the world.

the most   tree alive.

12 **Read the answers. Write the questions.**

1. <u>Which species is one of the most endangered species in the Americas?</u>

    The armadillo is one of the most endangered species in the Americas.

2. _____

    The piranha has the sharpest teeth of all fish.

3. _____

    The white millipede has the most legs of any animal. It has a total of 750 wiggling legs!

4. _____

    The land mammal with the fewest teeth is the narwhal. It has only two, large teeth.

13 Write the words in the correct category. Then listen and check your answers.

algae	carnivore	herbivore
nectar	nutrient	protein

Words that describe animals	Words that describe plants	Words that describe food
carnivore		

14 Read. Then answer the questions.

How to Take Care of a Pitcher Plant

If your parents won't allow pets in your home, you could try growing a pitcher plant. It could be your perfect "pet plant". You can take care of it and feed it just like a pet. But be careful. At mealtime, these plants get very hungry! So hungry they could eat a rat! Yes, this plant is the largest meat-eating plant in the world. In fact, pitcher plants can grow up to three feet—that's one meter—tall!

Pitcher plants need lots of nutrients and protein. To be a good pitcher plant owner, you will have to make sure that your plant gets lots of sunlight and water. These are important to keep your little carnivore happy and healthy. Water is especially important. It makes the top of the plant slippery so that bugs can slip into the nectar. The nectar helps the plant digest the food.

Check your plant to make sure it is catching enough bugs. Some days you will have to feed it an extra bug or two if it looks hungry. Your pitcher plant will have the most healthy and happiest pet plant life of all if you love and take good care of it.

1. What is unusual about the pitcher plant?

_____

2. How can you make a pitcher plant a healthy plant?

_____

3. Would you like to own a pitcher plant? Would it make a good pet?

_____

15 Read the words in the box and look at the chart. Then listen and write the words in the correct place.

| Arabic zero (0) | calendar | chocolate | democracy | herbal remedies |
| myths | number system | Olympic Games | terraced farming | |

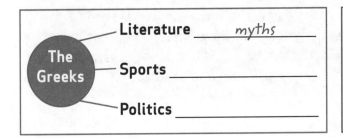

Literature ___myths___

The Greeks — Sports _____

Politics _____

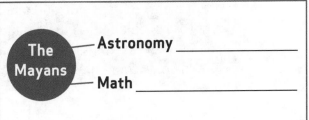

The Mayans — Astronomy _____

Math _____

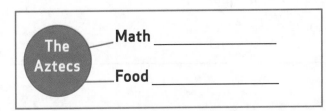

The Aztecs — Math _____

Food _____

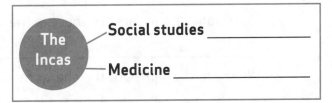

The Incas — Social studies _____

Medicine _____

16 Which ancient civilization should you thank for things you have today? Read and write *The Greeks, The Aztecs, The Mayans,* or *The Incas.*

1. Your favorite soccer team can compete to be the best in the world at the Olympic Games.

   The Greeks

2. The people in Thailand and Vietnam grow rice and other crops on hills.

   _____

3. When you get hungry and want something sweet, you eat a chocolate bar.

   _____

4. When you get sick, your mom or doctor might give you herbal remedies to make you feel better.

   _____

5. When you get bored, you can read incredible stories about heroes, and gods and goddesses.

   _____

17 Think and write about one more thing that you should thank an ancient civilization for.

_____

_____

A play tells a story. Both a play and a story have ...

- Characters
- Important events
- An order of events

But a play is a special kind of story. It tells the story through dialogues and actors speaking those dialogues. The dialogues show what the people want, what they are thinking, and what is happening or has happened. The dialogue is the only thing that tells us about the characters and events.

18 **Read the story of Daedalus and Icarus in 5. Answer the questions.**

1. How many characters are there in the story?

_____

2. What are the names of the characters?

_____

3. How would you describe each of the characters?

_____

_____

4. There are three events mentioned in the story.

What happened first? _____

What happened second? _____

What happened in the end? _____

5. What do these characters say or think or wish in the story?

King Minos: _____

_____

Daedalus: _____

_____

Icarus: _____

_____

19 **On a separate piece of paper, rewrite one of the events as a play. Tell the story of the event in a dialogue between two of the characters. Use your notes in 18.**

20 Read and write.

1. Write an example of a prime number: _____
2. Write the name of a famous artist: _____
3. Write the name of a sport that is played in the Olympic Games: _____
4. Write the name of a famous playwright: _____

21 Read and complete the sentences with *more* or *fewer*.

1. A spider has eight legs. An ant has six.

   The spider has ____*more legs*____ than an ant.

2. I have two pets. My friend Alex has three pets.

   I have _____ than Alex.

3. New York City has about 8 million people. Los Angeles has almost 4 million people.

   New York City has _____ than Los Angeles.

4. My pitcher plant eats four bugs a day. Your pitcher plant eats six bugs a day.

   My pitcher plant eats _____ than yours.

22 Complete the sentences. Use *the least*, *the fewest*, or *the most* and the underlined words.

1. Vatican City is the world's smallest country. It has very few <u>people</u> living there.

   It *has the fewest people* _____ of any country in the world.

2. France has a lot of <u>pet owners</u>.

   It _____ of any European country.

3. Canada doesn't have many species of <u>mammals</u>.

   It _____ of any country in the world.

4. Approximately 32% of U.S. families own <u>dogs</u>. That is more than any other country.

   It _____ of any country in the world.

5. <u>People</u> do not live permanently in Antarctica.

   It _____ of any other continent.

Think Big

1 Look at Units 4, 5, and 6. Choose words from the units. Write them in the charts.

DREAMS FOR THE FUTURE

live in another country

_____

_____

_____

SUPERPOWERS

travel through time

_____

_____

_____

SCHOOL INTERESTS

prime numbers

_____

_____

_____

2 Make a list of your superheroes – real or imaginary.

3 Look at **2**. Choose one superhero and complete the chart about your choice.

His/Her Dreams

_____

_____

_____

His/Her Powers

_____

_____

_____

His/Her Interests

_____

_____

_____

4 Look at **1**, **2**, and **3**. Write a song about your superhero. Use some of these sentences in your song. Add your own sentences.

I'll save my best numbers for you.

If I could fly like Superman…

Pow! Bam! Slam! Kaboom!

Superhero, here I am.

I'll be living on the moon.

I've got my superpower.

I'll be traveling through time soon.

5 In Your Classroom

Work in pairs and share.

MYSTERIES

1 Match the pictures to the explanations of these unsolved mysteries. What do you think? Are these explanations possible? Circle your answer.

		Possible	**Not Possible**
___	Overnight, the wind creates unusual circles in farmer's fields.	**Possible**	**Not Possible**
___	Giant pre-historic ape-like men still live in the Himalayas of Asia.	**Possible**	**Not Possible**
___	Large, heavy rocks up to 300 kilos move from place to place by themselves.	**Possible**	**Not Possible**
___	The 246 page, 15th century book of drawings and strange letters was written as a hoax to fool people and it doesn't really mean anything.	**Possible**	**Not Possible**
___	Aliens from outer space created perfectly round sculptures in Costa Rica.	**Possible**	**Not Possible**

2 Complete the conversations. Then listen and correct your answers.

> explanation   Great Pyramids   Northern Lights   proof
> scientific   theories   unsolved

A: Have you ever heard about the _____?
(1)

B: I think so. They're those bright colorful lights in the night sky. They're the lights that shine off of the ice caps in the Arctic and Antarctica.

A: No, that was just a theory. Now there's _____
(2)

_____. Gases in the air cause these nighttime
(3)

fireworks.

A: The _____ in Egypt are incredible, aren't they?
(4)

B: They sure are. Does anyone have an _____ of how
(5)
they were built?

A: Well, some scientists have _____ about it, but the
(6)

mystery is still _____.
(7)

3 Read the sentences about the places in 2. Circle *True* or *False*. Correct the false sentences.

1. The Great Pyramids are an unsolved mystery, but scientists have some theories about them.   **True**   **False**

   _____

2. There is a scientific proof about how the Great Pyramids were built.   **True**   **False**

   _____

3. The Northern Lights appear in the night sky over Egypt.   **True**   **False**

   _____

4. There is a scientific explanation of what causes the Northern Lights.   **True**   **False**

   _____

25
4 **Listen and read. Then answer the questions.**

The Voynich Manuscript

The Voynich manuscript, written in the 15th century in Western Europe, is beautiful to look at. The pages of this "book" are full of colorful, lovely drawings of plants and astronomical objects, like suns and moons. The handwriting that surrounds the drawings appears to describe herbal remedies from plants. You can imagine that the author was a doctor or a scientist. But if you look more closely, you'll notice two very strange things: The words are not in any known language, and the plants do not exist. That's incredible, isn't it?

Scientists have studied the Voynich manuscript for years and have tried to understand the meaning of the words and the strange drawings. The words do follow some "rules" of a language, or even two languages, but scientists still cannot figure out what the language is. And they do not know where the author learned about the strange plants. An early theory was that the writer used an artificial language. Another theory was that the whole thing was a hoax. But why would someone spend so much time on a manuscript and work so hard if the manuscript was just a prank?

Today a group of scientists around the world are working together to create a machine that will help them finally crack the code. What do you think? Will a computer be able to help them understand the information that the 15th century writer so beautifully and carefully put into this manuscript?

COMMENTS (2)

This is fascinating! What theories do scientists have about the plants? Could the plants be extinct species? They're amazing!

Savvy Sam

I agree with Savvy Sam. The plants are cool. I wonder if the plants look different because they are ancient! Plants could change over time, right? I hope scientists crack the code soon. Maybe the manuscript contains the cure for diseases today. You never know!

Jazmin

1. How old is the Voynich manuscript?

_____

2. What is strange about the Voynich manuscript?

_____

5 Listen and read. Then circle *True* or *False*.

Tony: I got you <u>hooked on</u> Kryptos, didn't I?

Gerald: You sure did. I found lots of <u>cool stuff</u> about Kryptos. Did you know the creator of the codes has given more clues recently?

Tony: Seriously? What are the new clues?

Gerald: He gave six letters out of the 97 in the last phrase.

Tony: I bet the decoders got excited, didn't they?

Gerald: <u>Totally</u>. On the sculpture, the letters are NYPVTT. When decoded, the letters read *BERLIN*.

Tony: I can't imagine being a code breaker, can you? I wouldn't be able to sleep because I'd be thinking about it all the time.

Gerald: That's exactly what's happening. Many people are obsessed with cracking the code, and that's all they think of and do every day.

Tony: <u>That's insane</u>.

1. Gerald is really interested in Kryptos.	**True**	**False**
2. Gerald found out about Kryptos before Tony.	**True**	**False**
3. Tony knew about the new clues that the creator gave out.	**True**	**False**
4. Tony thinks a code breaker probably doesn't sleep much.	**True**	**False**

6 Match the expressions with the sentences. Write the letter.

___ **1.** I'm hooked on it.

___ **2.** Cool stuff.

___ **3.** Totally.

___ **4.** That's insane.

a. I agree with you completely.

b. That's crazy. It's unreasonable.

c. I'm obsessed with it.

d. Interesting things.

7 Complete the sentences with the expressions in 6. Then listen and check.

1. A: Jennifer's always studying.

    B: I know. She's _____ historical mysteries. She studies 24/7. All day, every day!

    A: Really? _____.

2. A: There's a craft fair on Saturday. Let's go. They always have such _____, don't they?

    B: _____. I could buy everything. Great idea!

Grammar

AFFIRMATIVE STATEMENTS	NEGATIVE TAGS	NEGATIVE STATEMENTS	POSITIVE TAGS
The geoglyphs **are** in Peru, Experts **can** explain them, We **love** mysteries,	**aren't** they? **can't** they? **don't** we?	Atlantis **isn't** real, Scientists **can't** find it, It **doesn't** make sense,	**is** it? **can** they? **does** it?

8 Complete the tag questions.

1. The Voynich Manuscript is a mystery, _____?

2. The plants in the manuscript aren't real species, _____?

3. Scientists can't figure out the language in the manuscript, _____?

4. The pictures of the plants are beautiful, _____?

5. The manuscript isn't a hoax, _____?

6. People can find a lot of information about the Voynich Manuscript online, _____?

9 Complete the sentences. Make tag questions.

1. Scientists don't have an explanation for the crop circles in England, _____?

2. The crop circles have perfect geometric patterns, _____?

3. The crop circle appears in fields overnight, _____?

4. Proof for the theory that aliens created crop circles doesn't exist, _____?

10 Unscramble the sentences. Make tag questions.

1. don't / some people / in the Bermuda Triangle / do / believe / they

   Some people don't believe in the Bermuda Triangle, do they?

2. don't / a mysterious / people / phenomenon / love / they

   _____

3. didn't / the Nazca Lines / learned / we / a lot about / my classmates and I

   _____

4. didn't / a theory for the Sailing Stones / did / scientists / have / for a long time / they

   _____

5. seem / the city of Atlantis / does / doesn't /real / it

   _____

11 Zack is writing a play about Atlantis. Help him complete the play. Use the tag questions in the box.

> didn't they?   don't we?   do they?
> isn't it?   wasn't he?   were they?

Tabitha: Well, here we are in the city of Atlantis! Wow! It's so cool,
1 _____

Bryan: Yeah. Look at that huge water fountain! It's beautiful!

Tabitha: We look a little funny wearing jeans and a T-shirt,
2 _____

Bryan: I told you that we would look strange. Look at that wall. It's covered in gold and silver!

Tabitha: All the walls are covered in metals. Scientists don't really know why this place disappeared, 3 _____

Bryan: No, but Plato seemed to know. He said that the gods destroyed Atlantis.

Tabitha: Right. The people weren't good, 4 _____ So, the gods destroyed the city with an earthquake and giant waves,5 _____

Bryan: That's right. Hey, look at that hill. Why is there a hill in the middle of the city?

Tabitha: Look at the top.

Bryan: Oh, that's right. That's the temple of Poseidon. He was a very scary god,
6 _____

Tabitha: Totally. It sure is fun to travel back in time.

12 Listen and read. Then complete the diagram. Use the words in the box.

atom (3)	nitrogen (2)
oxygen	solar winds

What Causes the Aurora Borealis?

The Aurora Borealis is one of the most beautiful phenomena on Earth. It is also one of the most mystifying since every display of shimmering colors, lines, and shapes is different every time it appears. Long ago, people in Finland thought the lights came from a mystical fox flashing its tail in the sky. The Algonquin tribe in Canada thought that the lights came from the god that created them. They believed that after the god finished, he went up north to live. The god showed his love for his people by making large spectacular fires that his people could see and enjoy.

Then in 2008, scientists developed a theory that everyone could agree on. The spectacular lights were caused by the solar wind blowing around ions, atoms, gases, and other things in the atmosphere, and making them collide. When they collided, they produced the colorful displays of light. So, how does it actually happen? The exact process is complicated, but perhaps this simple diagram can help.

The hot solar winds from the sun are blowing the oxygen and two nitrogen atoms around. The atoms are full of energy. When they collide, they give off colors. Oxygen produces a yellow-green to brownish red color. The two nitrogen atoms produce different colors. Ionic nitrogen atoms produce a blue color. Neutral nitrogen atoms produce red and purple colors.

This is a simple explanation of how the Aurora Borealis is made. It is good to understand the science behind the phenomenon, but the myths are fun to know too, aren't they?

13 Read. Then answer the questions.

Huge, Hairy Ape-like Creatures: Real or Hoax?

Huge, hairy ape-like creatures have been the "stars" of at least ten movies in Hollywood over the years. In some movies, the hairy creature is friendly and huggable, like a teddy bear. In other movies, it is a terrifying beast that wants to destroy everyone and everything. In real life, this creature has several names, depending on which region of the world it is seen in. In the United States and Canada, the creature is called Bigfoot or Sasquatch. In the Himalayas of Asia it is called the Yeti or the Abominable Snowman. The color of the fur may be different (the Yeti usually has white fur, and Bigfoot has dark brown or black), but they both appear to be up to nine feet tall and weigh from 700 to 900 pounds. Their feet can be as large as 17 inches long. But are these creatures real?

For years, scientists have thought that these creatures were a hoax, but to this day people continue to claim that they have seen them. In 2012, there were many sightings in the United States. One person posted his video on YouTube, and the video was seen more than 2 million times.

A theory of some scientists is that the creature is a Gigantopithecus, a giant ape-like species that scientists thought was extinct. There has not been any proof for this theory, but the mystery may soon be solved. Scientists think they have some DNA samples from sightings. If the tests are positive, then the mystery creatures will finally become part of the amazing, fascinating world of science. If they are negative, these creatures will be part of myths and legends. Whatever the result, it seems clear that these creatures will continue to appear in real-life sightings, in stories, and in movies. Why? Because we love mystery and fantasy, and we love to be surprised—at times, even frightened!—by the world around us.

1. Scientists think that the Yeti and Bigfoot are the same creature. Why do you think they look different in different regions of the earth?

   _____

   _____

2. Do you like to watch movies that have creatures like Bigfoot or the Yeti? Why or why not?

   _____

   _____

One purpose for writing is to explain something. When you write a cause-and-effect paragraph, you explain *why* something happens.

- Why something happens is called a **cause**.
- The thing that happens is called an **effect**.

For example, the aurora borealis is a beautiful display of lights. The beautiful lights are an effect. Why do the lights happen? That's the cause.

14 Read the paragraph. <u>Underline</u> the causes. (Circle) the effects.

> The aurora borealis is a brilliant light show. Colored bands of light paint the night sky in certain parts of the world. What makes this happen? Solar winds interact with the upper part of the atmosphere, causing atoms of oxygen and nitrogen to become charged. As the atoms return to their normal state, they give off colors.

15 Write a cause-and-effect paragraph about something that happened to you or something you read about in your science or social studies class. Use the chart below to organize your ideas.

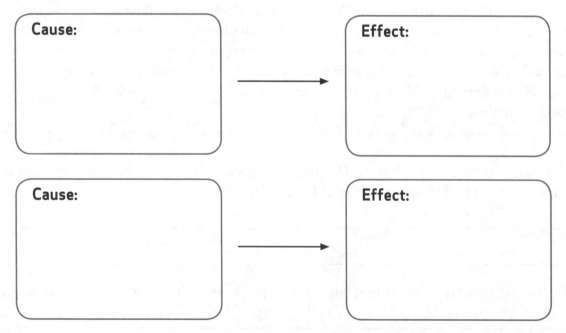

Cause:

Effect:

Cause:

Effect:

16 Complete the sentence. Circle the answer.

1. There is no ___ for planes and boats disappearing in the Bermuda Triangle.

   a. theory   **b.** phenomenon

2. Scientists know how the Sailing Stones moved. That mystery is ___.

   a. solved   **b.** unsolved

3. Scientists think that crop circles are a hoax. This is a ___.

   a. proof   **b.** theory

4. Code breakers won't stop trying to crack the code until they have ___ proof that the Voynich manuscript really is a hoax.

   a. solved   **b.** scientific

17 Correct the tag questions.

1. The Aurora Borealis is a phenomenon in the Northern hemisphere, is it?

   _____

2. The Yeti lives in the Himalayas in Asia, isn't it?

   _____

3. There is proof that the Sailing Stones are real, aren't there?

   _____

4. The people in the CIA want to challenge code breakers, didn't they?

   _____

5. Kryptos isn't a video game, isn't it?

   _____

18 Complete the dialogues. Use tag questions. Use the information you have learned about mysteries.

A: _____?

B: Yes, they are! That's true!

A: _____?

B: Yes, it is. I agree! Absolutely!

WHY IS IT FAMOUS?

1 Do you recognize these places? Match the descriptions with the pictures. Write the number. Why are these places famous? What do you think? Circle 1 for *architecture*, 2 for *natural beauty*, or 3 for *mystery*. You can circle more than one.

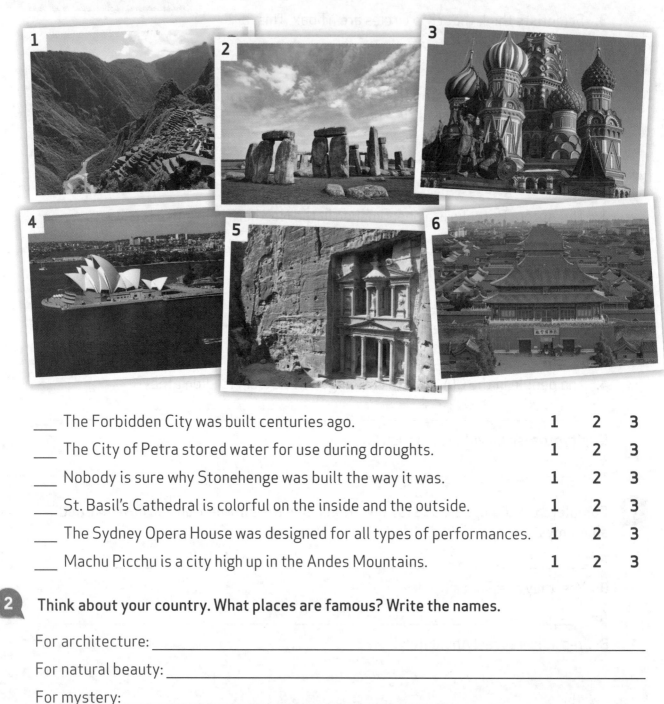

___ The Forbidden City was built centuries ago.	1	2	3
___ The City of Petra stored water for use during droughts.	1	2	3
___ Nobody is sure why Stonehenge was built the way it was.	1	2	3
___ St. Basil's Cathedral is colorful on the inside and the outside.	1	2	3
___ The Sydney Opera House was designed for all types of performances.	1	2	3
___ Machu Picchu is a city high up in the Andes Mountains.	1	2	3

2 Think about your country. What places are famous? Write the names.

For architecture: _____

For natural beauty: _____

For mystery: _____

3 Listen and label the pictures with the words from the box.

> mausoleum   monument   pyramid
> statue   temple   tower

1. _____

2. _____

3. _____

4. _____

5. _____

6. _____

4 Answer the questions.

1. Look at 3. If your class could travel to one of the places or structures, which one would you like to see? Why?

_____

_____

2. Have you ever visited an historic place like those pictured? What do you remember most about that place?

_____

_____

3. There are many beautiful places and structures in the world. Why do you think some places become famous and some do not?

_____

_____

5 Listen and read. Then answer the questions.

The Forbidden City

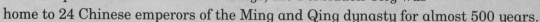

In the middle of Beijing, China, is the magnificent Forbidden City. Although now a museum and officially renamed the Palace Museum, or "Gugong" in Chinese, the Forbidden City was built in the early 1400s by Emperor Yongle as his imperial home. With 90 palaces and over 900 buildings, the Forbidden City was home to 24 Chinese emperors of the Ming and Qing dynasty for almost 500 years.

The Forbidden City is protected by a moat, and a wall that is almost 8 meters high. There is an inner court with buildings and rooms for the emperor and his family, and an outer court with halls and gardens where the emperor did his work and entertained guests. Only people invited by the emperor were allowed into the palace. All others were forbidden to enter.

In front of the main gate, there is a pair of bronze lions. The male lion is holding a globe, symbolizing the power of the emperor. The female lion has a baby cub. She symbolizes the health and happiness of the emperor's family.

The colors yellow and red appear everywhere. Roofs of the buildings and bricks of the floor are yellow. Yellow symbolized the royal family and its supreme importance to the world. Doors, windows, pillars, and walls were often red. Red symbolized happiness and celebration.

Today, people come from all over the world to see the thousands of items in the Palace Museum: paintings, ceramics, jade pieces, clocks, jewelry, and sculptures—all give us a glimpse of history. In 1987, the United Nations Educational, Scientific and Cultural Organization (UNESCO) included the Forbidden City on its World Heritage List for its incredible architectural beauty and wealth of cultural artifacts.

1. When was the Forbidden City built? Why was it built?

   _____

2. Why do you think the emperor's palace was called the Forbidden City?

   _____

3. There are statues of lions in front of the main gate. If you lived in a place like the Forbidden City, what animal statues would you have in front of your main gate? Why?

   _____

4. The colors red and yellow appear everywhere in the Forbidden City. If you lived in a place like the Forbidden City, what two colors would you use? What would they symbolize?

   _____

6 Listen and read. Then answer the question.

Tania: Hey, Eric! You're from Australia, right?

Eric: Yeah. I was born in Sydney. Why?

Tania: Well, I have to give a presentation in my art class. What do you know about the Sydney Opera House?

Eric: Quite a lot, actually. Did you know that the Opera House <u>is known for</u> its design?

Tania: Oh—yeah. <u>That makes sense</u>. I've seen pictures and it's amazing, isn't it?

Eric: Yeah, it's a <u>work of art</u>! I don't know who designed it, but I do know where the person was from. A design contest <u>was held</u> sometime in the 1950s, and the person who won was from Denmark.

Tania: Really! You know, it looks like a big boat, doesn't it?

Eric: Yeah, I've heard other people say the same thing. It's awesome!

Tania: Thanks, Eric. You've given me a good start.

Do Tania and Eric like the design of the Opera House? How do you know?

_____

7 Look at 6. Read the underlined expressions. How can you say them in other words? Match the expressions. Write the letter.

___ **1.** known for   **a.** happened or took place

___ **2.** That makes sense.   **b.** painting, sculpture, or object that is skillfully made

___ **3.** work of art   **c.** famous for

___ **4.** was held   **d.** That's logical. It's easy to understand.

8 Complete the sentences with the expressions in 7. Then listen and check.

1. A: My family is going to the city of Puebla this weekend.

   B: Really? I've heard of it, but I don't know much about it.

   A: It's _____ its architecture and arts and crafts. You should go!

2. A: How was your vacation in Paris?

   B: Great! We saw the Eiffel Tower. It's a phenomenal _____!

3. A: I'm doing research on Machu Picchu since we're going there on our next vacation.

   B: _____.

Grammar

Active	Passive
Archaeologists discovered Machu Picchu in 1911.	Machu Picchu **was discovered** in 1911 (by archaeologists).

9 Complete the sentences with the passive form of the verb in parentheses and *is/are*.

1. The Galapagos Islands _____ are known _____ (know) for their unique variety of animal and plant species.

2. The Forbidden City _____ (fill) with beautiful paintings and artifacts.

3. The Taj Mahal _____ (make) of marble.

4. The walls of the Taj Mahal _____ (decorate) with many floral designs.

5. The inside walls of St. Basil's Cathedral _____ (paint) every few years.

6. The Sydney Opera House _____ (locate) in Australia.

10 Next to each sentence, write *A* for *active* or *P* for *passive*.

_P_ **1.** Easter Island was discovered by Dutch explorers in 1722.

___ **2.** Scientists still don't know why the Moai statues on Easter Island were created.

___ **3.** Scientists believe that trees were used to move the statues on Easter Island.

___ **4.** Ivan the Terrible built St. Basil's Cathedral in Moscow in the mid-16th century.

___ **5.** The city of Petra was constructed sometime around the 4th century, B.C.E.

___ **6.** A Danish architect designed the Sydney Opera House.

11 Write sentences with the passive form of the verb.

1. call: El Castillo / the Pyramid at Kukulcan

_____

2. rebuild: some of the stones of Stonehedge / in the early 20th century

_____

3. give: The Statue of Liberty / to the United States as a gift

_____

> Leonardo da Vinci is the famous artist and inventor **who painted** the Mona Lisa.
> The Eiffel Tower is a landmark **that has become** the symbol of Paris, France.

12 Write *who* or *that*.

1. The Galapagos Islands are named after the huge tortoises _____ are native to the island.

2. Charles Darwin studied the plants and animals _____ lived on the Galapagos Islands in the early 1800s.

3. It was Charles Darwin _____ made the Islands famous.

4. The tortoises and lizards are not afraid of the visitors _____ come to see them.

5. The animal _____ is the best known of all is the Galapagos Tortoise.

13 Match the sentences. Write the letter.

___ **1.** Machu Picchu is an ancient city.

___ **2.** Many tourists get to Machu Picchu by walking on paths.

___ **3.** Scientists don't know much about the Incans.

___ **4.** Scientists know about the Spanish conquerors.

a. They invaded the city in the 1500s.

b. The city was built high in the Andes Mountains.

c. The Incans lived long ago in Machu Picchu.

d. The paths lead to the ancient city.

14 Look at 13. Rewrite the matching sentences as one sentence.

1. _Machu Picchu is an ancient city that was built high in the Andes Mountains._

2. _____

3. _____

4. _____

15 Listen and read. Then answer the questions.

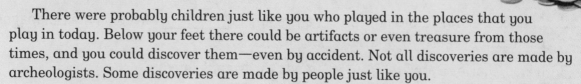

ACCIDENTAL DISCOVERIES

Do you ever wonder what the world around you looked like hundreds or even thousands of years ago? What do you know about the people and cultures that used to live where you live now?

There were probably children just like you who played in the places that you play in today. Below your feet there could be artifacts or even treasure from those times, and you could discover them—even by accident. Not all discoveries are made by archeologists. Some discoveries are made by people just like you.

One accidental discovery occurred in 1992, in England. A farmer was working in the fields when he lost his hammer. He asked a neighbor to help him find it. His neighbor had a metal detector. The first thing the metal detector found was a silver spoon. Then it found some jewelry and gold coins. The surprised farmers asked for the help of archeologists. When the archeologists came, they were shocked to discover a large box with over 14,000 Roman gold and silver coins inside. They believed that the treasure came from the fourth and fifth centuries B.C.E. The archeologists found other artifacts as well, including the farmer's hammer. The artifacts were sold to museums, and the farmers received 4 million dollars!

In another accidental discovery, workers in Wyoming, in the United States, were digging up land to make a soccer field. They discovered artifacts from an ancient village that existed as long ago as the first century C.E.

Do you think the past is just waiting for you to uncover it? It may be. So, the next time you walk out your door, look carefully at the world around you. You never know what you might find.

1. What did the farmer discover?

_____

2. What did archeologists determine?

_____

3. What accidental discovery was made in Wyoming?

_____

4. Is it possible for you to find artifacts from a long time ago? Why or why not?

_____

5. Look at the things you play with and the objects you use in your daily life. Pretend the year is 2500. Make a list of three objects that you want archaeologists to find and tell why each object is important in your life.

_____

16 Read and answer the questions.

The New 7 Wonders of the World

   Over two thousand years ago in ancient Greece, engineer Philon of Byzantium, created a list of the Seven Ancient Wonders of the World. Today, only one of those wonders still exists: the pyramids of Egypt. In 1999, Bernard Weber, a Swiss adventurer, decided to create a new list of world wonders. He began the New 7 Wonders Foundation. This time, he wanted people from all around the world to choose the seven new wonders that exist today. He asked people to send in their votes for the new wonders. People voted by texting, voting online at the website, and calling in their votes. By 2007, more than 100 million people had voted. Who were these voters? Most of the voters were not adults. Bernard Weber is proud of the fact that they were mostly children and young people.

   Weber and a group of people reviewed all the votes. They chose the new seven wonders based on these criteria:

- The places should each have a unique beauty.
- The places should come from all over the world and represent people from all over the world.
- The places should be from different environments, such as deserts and rainforests.
- The places should be important to people from different cultures.
- The places should be located on many continents.

   The final list of seven new wonders was decided. They are described on page 101 of your Student Book. Weber was delighted by the enthusiasm and love that people showed for their cultures and other cultures. This enthusiasm and love, he believes, creates a feeling of hope for the future.

1. Who began the New 7 Wonders Foundation?

_____

2. Who voted for the new seven wonders?

_____

3. What does Weber say creates a feeling of hope for the future?

_____

17 Pretend that you have to choose seven special places in your town or city. What seven places are important to you, your family, and friends? Write about them and tell why.

_____

_____

When you do research for a report, use an idea web to organize the information in categories. For example, if you write about a country, make categories for its location, population, and important cities.

When you write, make sure that you write only about one category of information in each paragraph.

18 Look at the facts. Write the number of each fact in the correct category.

(1) between Pakistan and Burma

(2) Kolkata, Chennai, Bangalore, Mumbai

(3) southern Asia

(4) Hindi

(5) English – important language

(6) New Delhi – capital city

(7) one billion people

(8) seventh largest country in the world

The Republic of India

General Facts and Location	Population, People and Languages
1	

Major Cities

_____
_____
_____

19 The paragraph below should only include information about general facts and location of India. Circle the two sentences that do NOT belong in the paragraph.

The Republic of India is the seventh largest country in the world. It is located in southern Asia. Hindi is its national language. It is situated between Pakistan and Burma. It is the seventh largest country in the world. English is an important language, too.

20 Write a report about India. Write three paragraphs. In paragraph 1, write about general facts and location. In paragraph 2, write about major cities. In paragraph 3 write about population, people, and languages. Use information in 18 and 19. Add information from your own research and your own idea web.

21 Complete the sentences. Circle the letter.

1. A ___ is a place that is built for someone who has died.

   a. tower   **b.** mausoleum

2. The French gave the United States a ___ as a sign of friendship.

   a. statue   **b.** palace

3. There are famous ___ in both Egypt and Mexico.

   a. mausoleums   **b.** pyramids

4. In Indonesia, there is a ___ that has more than 500 statues of the Buddha.

   a. mausoleum   **b.** temple

22 Complete the statements with the passive form of the verbs.

> build   discover   locate   make   use

1. The Temple of Borobudur _____ by thousands of workers between 750 and 850 c.e.

2. The Taj Mahal _____ in Agra, India.

3. The Taj Mahal _____ of white marble.

4. Victoria Falls _____ by David Livingstone in 1855.

5. Some scientists believe that ropes _____ to pull the large Moai Statues across Easter Island.

23 Combine the sentences. Use *that* or *who* and the sentences in the box.

> They belonged to King Tut.
> They constructed the Taj Mahal.
> They lived on Easter Island.

1. In Agra, India, there were more than 22,000 people.

   _____.

2. The Rapa Nui are Polynesian people.

   _____.

3. In the Cairo Museum in Egypt are artifacts.

   _____.

unit 9 THAT'S ENTERTAINMENT!

1 Read the statements. Circle the ones that describe you.

1. Music is very important in my life.
2. Reading is very important in my life.
3. Video games are very important in my life.
4. Movies are very important in my life.
5. I like to read about singers and actors.
6. I like animation more than regular movies.
7. I like movies that scare me.
8. I like to talk about the concerts I go to.

2 Read and circle.

	Sometimes	Often	Never
1. I go to movie theaters.	S	O	N
2. I go to live concerts.	S	O	N
3. I go to bookstores or the library.	S	O	N
4. I go to festivals to see people dance.	S	O	N
5. I watch movie award shows on TV.	S	O	N
6. I watch music contests on TV.	S	O	N
7. I read when I get bored.	S	O	N
8. I play video games when I get bored.	S	O	N

3 Complete the sentences. Use the words in the box.

> book signing   comic book exhibition   concert
> festival   movie premiere   video-game launch

1. People are walking around dressed up as Star Wars storm troopers, and Avatar characters, and Mario. There are cool books, posters, T-shirts, and hats for sale. Going to a _____ is so much fun!

2. People are standing in line waiting until midnight to get in the store. Everybody wants to be the first to own the new game. This _____ is the best!

3. The place is full of people dancing and singing along with the performer on stage. The music is really loud! The tickets were expensive, but worth it to see this singer in _____!

4. Photographers are taking pictures of the actors as they walk into the theater. People are so excited to see their favorite stars! Being at a _____ is incredible!

5. The author of the latest best-selling book is sitting behind a table. People are standing in line holding the book. A _____ is really fun to go to.

6. Thousands of people have come to see the dancers dressed in stunning traditional costumes dancing to folk music. People are in a wonderful mood for these two days at the _____.

4 Answer the questions.

1. If you went to a comic book exhibition and you could dress as any character what character would you be? Why?

   _____

2. If you could be a famous author, singer, or actor, which one would you be? Why?

   _____

5 Read and listen. Then read the statements and circle the correct names.

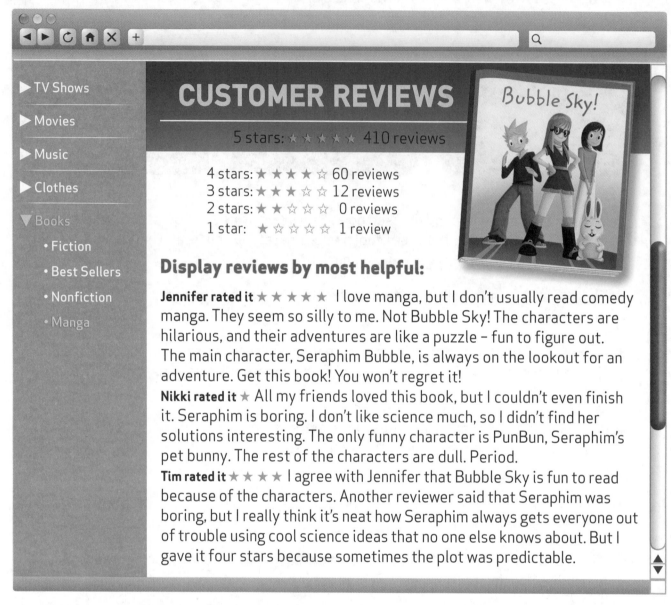

CUSTOMER REVIEWS

Bubble Sky!

5 stars: ★ ★ ★ ★ 410 reviews

4 stars: ★ ★ ★ ☆ 60 reviews
3 stars: ★ ★ ☆ ☆ 12 reviews
2 stars: ★ ☆ ☆ ☆ 0 reviews
1 star: ★ ☆ ☆ ☆ 1 review

TV Shows
Movies
Music
Clothes
Books
• Fiction
• Best Sellers
• Nonfiction
• Manga

Display reviews by most helpful:

Jennifer rated it ★ ★ ★ ★ ★ I love manga, but I don't usually read comedy manga. They seem so silly to me. Not Bubble Sky! The characters are hilarious, and their adventures are like a puzzle – fun to figure out. The main character, Seraphim Bubble, is always on the lookout for an adventure. Get this book! You won't regret it!

Nikki rated it ★ All my friends loved this book, but I couldn't even finish it. Seraphim is boring. I don't like science much, so I didn't find her solutions interesting. The only funny character is PunBun, Seraphim's pet bunny. The rest of the characters are dull. Period.

Tim rated it ★ ★ ★ ★ I agree with Jennifer that Bubble Sky is fun to read because of the characters. Another reviewer said that Seraphim was boring, but I really think it's neat how Seraphim always gets everyone out of trouble using cool science ideas that no one else knows about. But I gave it four stars because sometimes the plot was predictable.

1. **Jennifer / Nikki / Tim** said that the characters were hilarious.

2. **Jennifer / Nikki / Tim** said that all her friends loved the book.

3. **Jennifer / Nikki / Tim** said that sometimes the plot was predictable.

6 Answer the questions.

1. Why did Jennifer like the adventures?

_____

2. Have you ever read manga? What would a manga book need to include for you to give it five stars?

_____

7 Listen and read. Then answer the questions.

Ann: Mom? Um, could I possibly borrow ten dollars?

Mom: What for?

Ann: I want to go and see all the celebrities at the movie premiere of Spider-Man. All my friends are going. But I don't have enough money for the train.

Mom: What happened to your allowance?

Ann: I spent it to go to that concert last week. It was more expensive than I thought.

Mom: Well, I suppose I could give you next week's allowance in advance, but that means you won't get anything next week.

Ann: OK. Deal! Thanks, Mom.

1. What does Ann want from her mom?

_____

2. Ann won't get an allowance next week. Why?

_____

8 Look at 7. Circle the correct answer.

1. When Mom says "What for?" she means ___.

   a. Why do you need it?   **b.** What do you mean?

2. "In advance" means ___.

   a. an increase   **b.** early

3. When Ann says "Deal!" she means ___.

   a. I agree.   **b.** Let's play cards.

9 Complete the dialogue with an underlined word in 7. Listen and check your answer.

Juan: Do you want to stop at the store on the way home?

Jim: ¹_____

Juan: I need some things for my science project.

Jim: OK. But only if you stop with me at the pizza place next door. I'm so hungry!

Juan: OK. ²_____

Grammar

Direct speech	Reported speech
Claire said, "The album **isn't** as good as the last one."	Claire said (that) the album **wasn't** as good as the last one.
Josh said, "I **am going** to the premiere."	Josh said (that) he **was going** to the premiere.

10 Read the dialogues and answer the questions. Use reported speech.

Katie: Hey Joe! What are you doing tonight?

Joe: I'm going to a live show at Dragon's Den to see One Direction. What about you?

Katie: I'm not doing anything.

1. What is Joe doing tonight?

   He said he was going to a live show at Dragon's Den to see One Direction.

2. What is Katie doing tonight?

   _____

Sam: The new Play to Win 2 video game is really challenging.

Zena: It's much better than Play to Win 1.

3. What did Sam say about Play to Win 2?

   _____

4. What did Zena say about Play to Win 2?

   _____

Nina: I want to go to the comic book exhibition!

John: Me, too! I'm going to dress up as Mario.

5. Where did Nina want to go?

   _____

6. What did John say?

   _____

11 Read the dialogues and complete the sentences. Use reported speech.

> I don't want to miss the book signing at the bookstore today. My mom is taking me.

> I'm so excited. I'm going with my friend to a video-game launch today!

1. He _said_ he _didn't want_ to miss the book signing.

2. He _____ his mom _____ him.

3. She _____ she _____ so excited.

4. She _____ she _____ to a video-game launch.

12 Read the dialogue and answer the questions. Use reported speech.

Janet: Hi, Chuck. Where are you going?

Chuck: I'm going to the movies with a friend.

Janet: You're lucky. My friend doesn't want to go with me. I don't want to go alone. But I really want to see the new Bubble Sky movie.

Chuck: Come with us.

Janet: Seriously? Thanks!

1. What did Chuck say about his plans?

   He said he was going to the movies with a friend.

2. What did Janet say about her friend?

   _____ with her.

3. What did she say about going to the movies alone?

   _____

4. What did she say she wanted to do?

   _____

13 Match the words and meaning. Draw lines.

1. arcade
2. compete
3. graphics
4. scores

a. try to win at something
b. pictures or images
c. the number of points a player gets in a game
d. a special room or building where people go to play video games

14 Listen and read. Then answer the questions.

Video Games: The Year 2000 and Now

The changes to the computer and video games industry since the year 2000 have been incredible. New technology has changed how, where, and what people play, as well as who they play with. We have a lot more choices now than we used to.

How People Play and Who They Play With

In the year 2000, people played on game consoles or desktop computers or in arcades. When they wanted to play with others, they invited them over to their house, or they played alone. Some online games were available at the end of the 1990s, but they were expensive and not as many people had access to the Internet. Today people can play games anywhere they want on portable devices, like gaming devices, phones, or tablets. They can play online with friends or even with other players from around the world.

What People Play

Games today have graphics that are sharper and more life-like than they used to be, and new technology has made games more challenging, with more variety. Since 2000, Massively Multi-player Online games (MMOs) have become popular. People like to compete against each other for higher scores. They love virtual worlds that offer experiences they could never have in real life. Dancing and exercise games and sports and adventure games have also become more popular.

This trend towards more choices and deeper involvement in virtual worlds will continue to change video games well into the future.

1. How is playing video games in 2000 different from playing video games today?

_____

2. Why do people like MMO games?

_____

3. Do you have a favorite video game? What is it? Why do you like it?

_____

15 Read. Then answer the questions.

Unique Musical Instruments

Every culture has musical instruments that are unique to its culture. The instruments are often made from a variety of materials, such as wood, steel, animal bones, and plastic. There is an orchestra in Vienna that is very unique because it plays instruments made from the things your mother tells you to eat every day. The Vienna Food Orchestra plays instruments made out of vegetables.

The eleven musicians in the Vienna Food Orchestra play carrot flutes, radish coronets, bell pepper rattlers, carrot trumpets, eggplant clappers, pumpkin bongos, and cucumber phones. The orchestra plays contemporary music, jazz, and electronic music, among others. They have been playing together since 1998. They play concerts around the world. At the end of their concerts, the audience members receive a bowl of vegetable soup to enjoy. Their third album is called Onionoise and includes songs entitled "Nightshades" and "Transplants."

Why did this group of visual artists, poets, designers, and writers choose vegetables to create music? They were fascinated by the challenge to produce musical sounds using natural foods. They constantly experiment with vegetables to create new sounds. As part of their work, they give workshops on how to create instruments from vegetables. A CBS morning show in the United States said it was "... a highly unusual, tasty musical performance."

You knew vegetables were good for you. Now you know that they sound good, too!

1. Would you go to a Vienna Food Orchestra concert? Why or why not?

   _____

   _____

2. If you could play one of the vegetable instruments, which one would you like to play? Why?

   _____

   _____

3. Read the list of instruments again. Think of two other vegetables that the Vienna Food Orchestra could use to make instruments. Tell why.

   _____

   _____

A good movie review briefly describes the important parts of the movie: the story, the hero and characters, your opinion (what you liked and didn't like).

Before you write, make a chart that includes these topics and use vivid adjectives, such as *stunning, captivating, tense, dull,* and *boring.*

When you write, order your ideas. Write about the story first, but don't tell the ending! Some people want the ending to be a surprise. Then write about the characters. Describe them and what they do. Finally, describe what you liked and didn't like (for example, the acting or special effects).

16 Put the paragraphs in order. Write 1, 2, 3.

Review of *Bubble Sky: the Movie*

____ Some of the acting is fabulous! Melinda Mendez is very good as Seraphim Bubble. Brad Davis is hilarious as Tran. The evil Ms. Doze, played by Vivian Bell, is captivating, but Sandy Dennis as the teacher is dull. The special effects are stunning! All in all, this was a very cool movie!

____ "Bubble Sky" is a captivating animation adventure. In the story, a young girl discovers that her middle school is taken over by aliens. She figures out that a particular herb might destroy them. She needs to find the herb and then get the aliens to eat it.

____ Seraphim Bubble is the hero of the story. Her pet rabbit, PunBun, gives good advice. Seraphim's younger brother Tran and her friend Gayle help her fight the aliens.

17 Look at 16. Complete the chart about Bubble Sky.

The story	The hero and characters	The opinion (what you liked and didn't like)

18 Write a review of a movie playing near you this weekend. Make a chart to help you.

19 Circle the correct events.

1. The author arrived late to the **movie premiere / book signing**. The manager of the bookstore was upset because people were waiting for a long time.

2. My brother and I went to the **comic book exhibition / video-game launch**. We dressed up as Mario and Pikachu. There were thousands of people there.

3. My town is having an arts and crafts **concert / festival**. For three days painters, potters, and jewelry makers will be selling their work.

4. This Friday night all the stars will be at the **movie premiere / festival** of the new Superman movie.

5. The **concert / launch** tickets for The Eyes go on sale next Tuesday. They will sell out fast!

20 Read and correct the one mistake in each reported speech sentence.

1. **Carol:**   I'm tired.

   Reported speech: She says she was tired.

   _____

2. **Jason:**   I'm going to be at the launch tomorrow.

   Reported speech: He said he is going to be at the launch tomorrow.

   _____

3. **Diana:**   I want to meet the author of the book.

   Reported speech: She said she want to meet the author of the book.

   _____

4. **Will:**   I don't like sci-fi movies.

   Reported speech: He said he doesn't like sci-fi movies.

   _____

21 Write the sentences using reported speech.

1. **Lara:** I'm a pretty good singer.

   _____

2. **Paolo:** I don't want to go to the festival today.

   _____

Think Big

1 Look at the pictures. Complete the names. Add your own names on the extra lines.

MYSTERIOUS EVENTS

1. Northern _____

2. _____ circles

3. Bermuda _____

4. _____

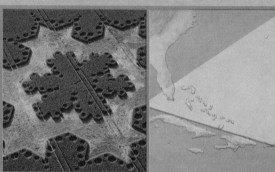

FAMOUS PLACES

1. _____ of Borobudur

2. _____ of Liberty

3. _____ of Kukulcan

4. _____

SPECIAL EVENTS

1. _____ signing

2. rock _____

3. movie _____

4. _____

2 Find a famous place or event that interests you. Complete the chart.

Name of the place or event	_____
When was it built, or discovered, or found? When did it take place? Where was it located?	_____ _____
Is this a place or event that was mentioned in a song? What is the name of the song? Who is the singer? What are the lines (the lyrics) that mention the place?	_____ _____ _____ _____
This place or event was described in a book, online, or in a magazine, wasn't it? What was the title of the book or article? What did the writer say about it?	_____ _____ _____

3 Do research. Find more information about the place or event that interests you in 2. Write a report about the place or event.

_____
_____
_____
_____
_____
_____

4 In Your Classroom

Work in pairs and share.

Read Nina's schedule for her science report. Write questions and answers.
Use *yet* and *already*.

The Importance of the Monarch Butterfly
by Nina Bunuel

Monday	Tuesday	Wednesday	Thursday	Friday
Morning: Go to Museum of Natural History, draw Monarch butterflies. Afternoon: Write questions about the butterflies.	Morning: Do research about Monarch butterflies and answer my questions.	Morning: Write my report on Monarch butterflies.	Morning: Create my presentation.	Morning: Hand in my report and give presentation.

1. *It's Monday afternoon.*

   Q: (Nina / go to the museum) <u>Has Nina gone to the museum yet</u> ?

   A: <u>Yes, she has. She has already gone to the museum.</u>

2. *It's Tuesday.*

   Q: (write / her report) _____?

   A: _____

3. *It's Tuesday afternoon.*

   Q: (she / do her research) _____?

   A: _____

4. *It's Thursday afternoon.*

   Q: (she / create her presentation) _____?

   A: _____

5. *It's Thursday afternoon.*

   Q: (she / give her presentation) _____?

   A: _____

1 Complete the sentences with the present perfect progressive form of the verbs and *for* or *since*.

1. Jimmy Woodard _____ (take) computers apart _____ he was five years old.

2. Caitlyn _____ (play) chess _____ she was very young.

3. Serena _____ (study) martial arts _____ five years.

4. I _____ (collect) baseball cards _____ two years.

2 Ask and answer questions about the chart. Use the present perfect and *for* or *since*.

Mr. Freedman's Class – Hobbies		
Student	**Hobby**	**How Long?**
Randy	collects coins	four years
Cynthia	makes jewelry	she was nine
David	draws anime characters	three years
Iris	takes dance classes	six months

1. How long <u>*has Randy collected coins?*</u> _____
   <u>*He's collected coins for four years.*</u> _____

2. How long _____ ?
   _____

3. _____ ?
   _____

4. _____ ?
   _____

1 Complete the sentences with the correct form of the verb in parentheses.

How will you help your family and friends?

1. If I _____ (finish) studying early, I'll help with the chores.
2. If my sister doesn't understand her homework, I _____ (help) her.
3. I _____ (call) my friend if he's sick.
4. If my dad _____ (ask) me to walk the dog, I _____ (do) it.
5. I _____ (tell) my parents if I _____ (break) something.

2 Complete the sentences.

1. If someone gives me a present, _____.
2. If someone in my family is sick, _____.
3. If my friend gets mad at me, _____.
4. If I don't feel well, _____.

3 Read and match. Write the letter.

Advice to a New Exchange Student in School

___ 1. You are new.

___ 2. Some people are mean to you.

___ 3. You don't speak the language well.

___ 4. You are always late for class.

a. Get organized so that you get to class on time.

b. Don't worry about your mistakes. Speak anyway.

c. Join clubs so that you meet people.

d. Stay away from those people.

4 Write the sentences in 3 with *should* or *shouldn't*.

1. *If you are new, you should join clubs so that you meet people.*
2. _____
3. _____
4. _____

5 Complete the sentences.

1. _____, you should ask them to stop.
2. _____, you should apologize.
3. _____, you should get help.

1 Read. Then circle the best answers.

	I like	I don't like
Emily	languages writing and blogging big families living close to family	sports
Al	making money all sports studying hard living in other countries	languages

1. In 10 years, **Emily / Al** will definitely be studying languages at college.

2. In 10 years, **Emily / Al** probably will be running and hiking on the weekends.

3. In 10 years, **Emily / Al** probably won't be living in the same city.

4. In 20 years, **Emily / Al** will definitely be running an international business.

5. In 20 years, **Emily / Al** probably will be writing books.

2 Read. Then complete the sentences with *I'll be* or *I won't be* and the words in parentheses.

What will you be doing in 20 years?

1. Celia: I love animals. I don't like living in the city. I like traveling.

   a. _I'll be working as a veterinarian._____ (work as a veterinarian)

   b. _____ (live in the country)

   c. _____ (take vacations to the same place every year)

2. Jeff: I love biology and helping people. I don't like cooking. I like boats. In 10 years,

   a. _____ (finish medical school)

   b. _____ (work as a chef)

   c. _____ (sail my boat)

3 Answer the questions about yourself. Use *No, definitely not, Yes, definitely, Probably not,* or *Yes, probably.*

1. In seven years will you be going to college? _____

2. In two years will you be blogging? _____

3. Next year will you be going to seventh grade? _____

1 Complete the dialogues. Use the phrases in the box.

> join some clubs   start a blog
> start reading fun things like manga   take lots of singing lessons

1. **Rita:** I want to be a singer when I grow up.

   Eddie: If I were you, _I'd take lots of singing lessons_ .

2. **John:** I don't enjoy reading.

   Nancy: If I were you, _____ .

3. **Tom:** I'm bored all the time.

   Kristy: If I were you, _____ .

4. **Grace:** I like writing a lot.

   Sam: If I were you, _____ .

2 Complete the sentences. Circle the correct verbs.

1. If you **will get / got** up earlier, you **wouldn't be / won't be** late for school all the time.

2. If the world **could have / can have** superheroes, it **would be / was** a safer place to live.

3. If he **practiced / will practice** guitar more, he **will play / would play** better.

4. If our chess team **will win / won** more games, we **will compete / would compete** in the state tournament.

3 Unscramble the phrases. Complete and answer the questions.

1. (live / could / you / if / anywhere)

   _____ ,

   where would you live?

   If I _____ .

2. (you / choose / which / would)
   If you could choose your own superpowers,

   _____ ?

   If _____ .

3. (didn't / if / have / computers / we)

   _____ ,

   what would we do?

   If _____ .

1 Complete the sentences. Circle the correct words.

1. Pandas only live in China. Brown bears live in many countries. Pandas live in **more** / **fewer** places than brown bears.

2. Brown bears spend **less** / **more** time eating than pandas. Pandas need to eat lots of bamboo every day to get enough nutrients.

3. Parakeets have **fewer** / **more** legs than dogs.

4. Parakeets eat **more** / **less** food than dogs.

2 Read the facts. Then complete the sentences using *most*, *least*, *fewest*, and the words in parentheses.

> **Facts**
> Monserrat has <u>less</u> crime than other countries.
> California has <u>more</u> people than other states.
> North America has <u>more</u> meat-eating plants than any other continent.
> Canada has very <u>few</u> species of mammals. It has fewer than any other country.
> People in Papua, New Guinea, speak <u>more</u> languages than people in other countries.
> Taki Taki, the language of Suriname, has <u>few</u> words.

1. California has the _____*most people*_____ of any other state in the U.S. (people)

2. People in Papua, New Guinea, speak the _____ of any country. (languages)

3. Canada has _____ of any country. (species of mammals)

4. North America has the _____ of any continent. (meat-eating plants)

5. The language of Taki Taki has the _____ of all languages. (words)

6. The country of Monserrat has the _____ of all countries. (crime)

3 Write sentences with the words in the box. Use superlatives.

1. The sun bear lives in Southeast Asia. It is only four feet tall. It is ____*the smallest bear*____ .

2. No bird is taller than the ostrich. The ostrich is _____ in the world.

3. No animal on land is larger than the elephant. The elephant is _____ on land.

4. No animal is louder than the blue whale. The blue whale is _____ in the world.

> large / creature
> loud / animal
> small / bear
> tall / bird

Unit 7 | Extra Grammar Practice

1 Complete the sentences. Write the correct word.

1. Kryptos is a sculpture at the CIA in the United States, _____ it?

   is   isn't

2. The fourth section of Kryptos isn't solved, _____ it?

   is   isn't

3. There are many people trying to solve it, _____ there?

   are   aren't

4. Code breakers can't solve it, _____ they?

   can   can't

5. Anyone can try to crack the code, _____ they?

   can   can't

2 Write tags to complete the questions.

1. The Great Pyramids of Egypt are beautiful, _____?

2. The Sailing Stones aren't a mystery anymore, _____?

3. The Bermuda Triangle is mysterious, _____?

4. You can climb the pyramids in Mexico, _____?

3 Unscramble the sentences and add words to make tag questions.

1. found out / scientists / in the early 20th century / about the Nazca Lines

   Scientists found out about the Nazca Lines in the early 20th century, didn't they?

2. the Nazcans created / the lines / don't / scientists / know why

   _____

3. drew / the Nazcans / animal and plant figures

   _____

4. the lines / need to see / you / from a plane

   _____

5. didn't know / you / about the Nazca Lines

   _____

1 Complete the sentences. Circle the correct verbs.

1. The Mona Lisa **paints** / **was painted** by Leonardo da Vinci.
2. The Taj Mahal **was built** / **built** by the emperor of India.
3. The Church of San Francisco de Asis in New Mexico **damaged** / **was damaged** by an earthquake in 1906.
4. The Statue of Liberty and the Eiffel Tower **were designed** / **designed** by the same French designer.

2 Write these sentences in the passive.

1. The people of Egypt built the Great Pyramids of Egypt.

   _____

2. Someone moved the moai statues of Easter Island.

   _____

3 Write sentences in the passive. Use the words in the box.

> carve   destroy   name   trade

1. The city of Petra, Jordan / one of the seven wonders of the world in 2007

   The city of Petra, Jordan, was named one of the seven wonders of the world in 2007.

2. The city of Petra / out of the sandstone mountains in the Jordan desert

   _____

   _____

3. Spices, perfumes, and other things / in Petra

   _____

   _____

4. The city of Petra / by an earthquake in 363 AD / nearly

   _____

   _____

4 Complete the sentences with the names of places in your country.

1. _____ is visited every year by thousands of tourists.
2. _____ is known as one of the most beautiful places in my country.
3. _____ is said to be one of the most mysterious places in my country.

1 What did the people say about the movie?
Change the sentences to reported speech.

Claire: The acting is incredible.

Jeff: The music is really cool.

Mira: It isn't the director's best film.

Nancy: It's definitely going to win an Oscar.

Todd: It's not that entertaining.

1. Claire _said the acting was incredible._

2. Jeff _____

3. Mira _____

4. Nancy _____

5. Todd _____

2 Change the sentences to reported speech.

Tina: I'm going to a Justin Bieber concert for my birthday.

Paul: I'm going to a movie premier featuring Jessica Alba.

1. Tina _said (that) she was going to a Justin Bieber concert for her birthday_ .

2. Paul _____ .

Michael: I want to buy the new Cats video game.

Sheila: I don't like playing video games.

3. Michael _____ .

4. Sheila _____ .

Tonya: I'm not going to the book signing.

Freddie: I always go to book signings.

5. She _____ .

6. He _____ .

My BIG ENGLISH World

1 **Make your own My Big English World book.**

1. Fold a piece of paper in half and make a 4-page book.

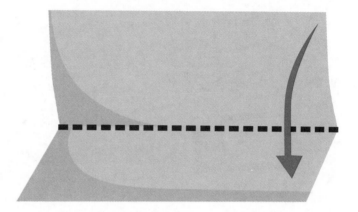

2. Make your own My Big English World book cover. Draw or paste your picture on your cover. Write your name, your age, and your class.

3. Look and listen around you every day. Open your My Big English World book. Write the title *English Around Me*. Draw, write, and paste things you see and hear in English. Write names, words, and sentences.

4. Close your book and make a back cover. Draw or write about interesting things you would like to remember from Big English.

In Your Classroom

ork in groups and share.

1 Complete the sentences. Circle the correct words.

1. Pandas only live in China. Brown bears live in many countries. Pandas live in **more** / **fewer** places than brown bears.

2. Brown bears spend **less** / **more** time eating than pandas. Pandas need to eat lots of bamboo every day to get enough nutrients.

3. Parakeets have **fewer** / **more** legs than dogs.

4. Parakeets eat **more** / **less** food than dogs.

2 Read the facts. Then complete the sentences using *most*, *least*, *fewest*, and the words in parentheses.

> **Facts**
> Monserrat has <u>less</u> crime than other countries.
> California has <u>more</u> people than other states.
> North America has <u>more</u> meat-eating plants than any other continent.
> Canada has very <u>few</u> species of mammals. It has fewer than any other country.
> People in Papua, New Guinea, speak <u>more</u> languages than people in other countries.
> Taki Taki, the language of Suriname, has <u>few</u> words.

1. California has the _____*most people*_____ of any other state in the U.S. (people)

2. People in Papua, New Guinea, speak the _____ of any country. (languages)

3. Canada has _____ of any country. (species of mammals)

4. North America has the _____ of any continent. (meat-eating plants)

5. The language of Taki Taki has the _____ of all languages. (words)

6. The country of Monserrat has the _____ of all countries. (crime)

3 Write sentences with the words in the box. Use superlatives.

1. The sun bear lives in Southeast Asia. It is only four feet tall. It is _____*the smallest bear*_____.

2. No bird is taller than the ostrich. The ostrich is _____ in the world.

3. No animal on land is larger than the elephant. The elephant is _____ on land.

4. No animal is louder than the blue whale. The blue whale is _____ in the world.

> large / creature
> loud / animal
> small / bear
> tall / bird

1 Complete the sentences. Write the correct word.

1. Kryptos is a sculpture at the CIA in the United States, _____ it?

   is   isn't

2. The fourth section of Kryptos isn't solved, _____ it?

   is   isn't

3. There are many people trying to solve it, _____ there?

   are   aren't

4. Code breakers can't solve it, _____ they?

   can   can't

5. Anyone can try to crack the code, _____ they?

   can   can't

2 Write tags to complete the questions.

1. The Great Pyramids of Egypt are beautiful, _____?
2. The Sailing Stones aren't a mystery anymore, _____?
3. The Bermuda Triangle is mysterious, _____?
4. You can climb the pyramids in Mexico, _____?

3 Unscramble the sentences and add words to make tag questions.

1. found out / scientists / in the early 20th century / about the Nazca Lines

   Scientists found out about the Nazca Lines in the early 20th century, didn't they?

2. the Nazcans created / the lines / don't / scientists / know why

   _____

3. drew / the Nazcans / animal and plant figures

   _____

4. the lines / need to see / you / from a plane

   _____

5. didn't know / you / about the Nazca Lines

   _____

1 Complete the sentences. Circle the correct verbs.

1. The Mona Lisa **paints** / **was painted** by Leonardo da Vinci.
2. The Taj Mahal **was built** / **built** by the emperor of India.
3. The Church of San Francisco de Asis in New Mexico **damaged** / **was damaged** by an earthquake in 1906.
4. The Statue of Liberty and the Eiffel Tower **were designed** / **designed** by the same French designer.

2 Write these sentences in the passive.

1. The people of Egypt built the Great Pyramids of Egypt.

   _____

2. Someone moved the moai statues of Easter Island.

   _____

3 Write sentences in the passive. Use the words in the box.

> carve   destroy   name   trade

1. The city of Petra, Jordan / one of the seven wonders of the world in 2007

   The city of Petra, Jordan, was named one of the seven wonders of the world in 2007.

2. The city of Petra / out of the sandstone mountains in the Jordan desert

   _____

   _____

3. Spices, perfumes, and other things / in Petra

   _____

   _____

4. The city of Petra / by an earthquake in 363 AD / nearly

   _____

   _____

4 Complete the sentences with the names of places in your country.

1. _____ is visited every year by thousands of tourists.
2. _____ is known as one of the most beautiful places in my country.
3. _____ is said to be one of the most mysterious places in my country.

1 What did the people say about the movie?
Change the sentences to reported speech.

Claire:	The acting is incredible.
Jeff:	The music is really cool.
Mira:	It isn't the director's best film.
Nancy:	It's definitely going to win an Oscar.
Todd:	It's not that entertaining.

1. Claire _said the acting was incredible._____
2. Jeff _____
3. Mira _____
4. Nancy _____
5. Todd _____

2 Change the sentences to reported speech.

Tina: I'm going to a Justin Bieber concert for my birthday.

Paul: I'm going to a movie premier featuring Jessica Alba.

1. Tina _said (that) she was going to a Justin Bieber concert for her birthday_____.
2. Paul _____.

Michael: I want to buy the new Cats video game.

Sheila: I don't like playing video games.

3. Michael _____.
4. Sheila _____.

Tonya: I'm not going to the book signing.

Freddie: I always go to book signings.

5. She _____.
6. He _____.

Workbook 6

My BIG ENGLISH
World

1 **Make your own My Big English World book.**

1. Fold a piece of paper in half and make a 4-page book.

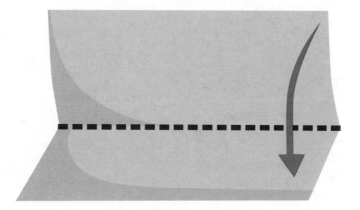

2. Make your own My Big English World book cover. Draw or paste your picture on your cover. Write your name, your age, and your class.

3. Look and listen around you every day. Open your My Big English World book. Write the title *English Around Me*. Draw, write, and paste things you see and hear in English. Write names, words, and sentences.

4. Close your book and make a back cover. Draw or write about interesting things you would like to remember from Big English.

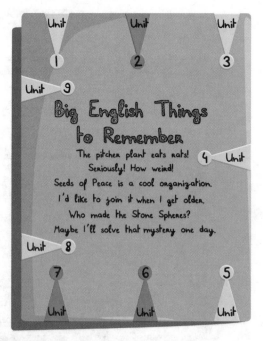

2 In Your Classroom

Work in groups and share.